CW00854524

Once Upon a Time in Russia
Memoirs of the Chief of
Criminal Investigation for the
Russian Empire

A. F. Koshko
Translated by S. Viatchanin

NEW YORK CONCEPT

Foreword

Age is not easy for me. Torn from my homeland, having lost many loved ones and forfeited my fortune, finally, after a long ordeal and wanderings, I found myself in Paris, where I dragged a greyish, aimless and useless life.

I do not live either in the present or in the future—I exist completely in the past, and only the memory of it keeps me going and gives me some moral satisfaction.

Thinking over each stage of my life, I can say that it was not spent in vain. My peers worked on the glorious task of building Russia, but the Bolshevik revolutionary storm, which destroyed my home, killed the results they had achieved by long, persistent and dedicated efforts. Russia died, and only the comfort of understanding that their work was meaningful stayed behind.

In this regard, I am happier than they. The fruits of my work benefited not the future of Russia, but were directly consumed by its people. With each arrest of a thief or capture of a murderer, I knew the results were obvious. I realized that by delaying and isolating such beasts as Sasha-Seminarians, Gilewicz or the killer of nine people in the Ipatiev alley, not only did I pay tribute to the victims, but also, what is more important, defended my citizens from streams of blood, which would inevitably have been spilled in the future by those dangerous criminals.

This consciousness remains with me today and supports me in the difficult days of my emigration.

It often happens now that tired after the working day, exhausted by the bum's rush of the subway, deafened by the roar of a thousand cars' horns, I return home, sit down into a comfortable

i

recliner, and images of the past begin to rise in my mind in the impending dusk.

I dream of Russia. I hear the Lenten bells of Moscow. Under the veil of elapsed years in exile, the past seems to me a welcome and bright sleep, where everything in it is dear and cute to me. With a condescending smile, I even remember many of you, my pitiful criminals . . . .

For this book, I have chosen 20 stories out of the galaxy of cases that took place during my long service in the office. I selected them consciously so as not to be repetitive, but to give the reader a series of samples that illustrate first how ingenious lawbreakers can be, and, second, the techniques needed to neutralize their intentions.

Of course, from an ethical side, some of the methods I used may seem dubious; still, to justify such practice, I want to remind you that the fight against the underworld is often coupled with deadly danger and can be successful only by use of weapons at least equal to theirs.

Anyway, is it possible to talk seriously about the strict application of ethical principles to those who could not care less about morality and elevated evil with all its vile manifestations to the status of a cult?

I wrote the stories from memory, and therefore, some inconsequential inaccuracies could be present.

I hasten, however, to assure the reader that my books do not have deliberate distortion of the facts or Pinkerton's elements like surprising twists to hook them up. Everything I tell you here is naked truth that occurred in the past and perhaps still lives in the memory of many.

I described these events to the best of my abilities and leave them to your judgement, my dear readers. Here are the grimaces, the ugly faces of real Russian life.

A. F. Koshko

Pink Diamond

One beautiful morning of 1913, I received a letter from a noble Moscow lady, Princess Shakhovsky-Glebov-Streshnev, one of the richest women in Russia, and in her letter the princess ardently asked me to visit her to discuss a very important matter. The sender's name was a guarantee of this matter being truly serious, so I departed immediately.

Back then the princess lived in one of her suburban manors near Moscow.

I found her agitated and upset. It turned out she had fallen a victim of a daring theft. There was a fireproof safe of quite primitive design in the bathroom next to her bedroom.

The princess had gotten used to keeping her jewels in it, especially those valuable to her because of family memories. Thus two strings of large pearls, a carnelian ring, and a pink diamond had disappeared from it. The carnelian ring's value was rather historical only, since under its stone there was a tiny lock of hair that once belonged to Eudoxia Lopukhina, the first wife of the Emperor Peter the Great. As is well-known, she ended her life in a monastery according to the will of her majestic husband. One of the Streshnevs was in love with the tsaritsa and managed to gain this precious souvenir from her. Since then the relic had passed in the Streshnevs family from father to son, and, at last, due to the termination of the male line, it had passed to the princess who summoned me.

The strings of pearls were simply of material value, but as for the pink diamond, it combined both: On the one hand, in old times it was given as a present by the Tsar Aleksey Mikhailovich to his wife (née Streshnev); on the other hand—it was a rarity in the kingdom of mineralogy.

The princess was extremely saddened by the loss of those dear things, but not any less agitated by the thought of the one responsible for it.

"It is bitter, endlessly bitter," she told me, "to be disappointed in people in general, and especially in those you had long been used to trust. Nevertheless, in this case I apparently have to drain this cup, since even with the most calm treatment of facts, with the most impartial analysis of what has happened, my suspicions do not scatter, but instead fall upon one person. I am talking about my French secretary, who has been living in my house for some 20 years. As flawless as his behavior was until now, you must nonetheless agree that the circumstances of this case are dramatically unfavorable for him: He was the only one who knew where the missing things were and had access to the safe. There's more to it: Yesterday all day he was out somewhere till late night, which happens extremely rarely with him, and, moreover, he stubbornly refuses to tell where he was between 7 and 11 o'clock in the evening. You must agree that it is more than strange!"

I found it necessary to invite the Frenchman to my office at the police station for interrogation. The secretary turned out to be an utterly nice person of around 45, calm and balanced. His face and his manners were not devoid of nobility. In short, he had this imprint on his appearance that is so characteristic for Frenchmen, the sons of a centuries- old culture.

He told me he was extremely surprised and saddened by the fact that the thought of his guilt could have occurred to the princess even for a minute, but at the same time he flatly refused to explain what he was doing the previous day, between 7 and 11 o-clock in the evening. As hard as I tried to convince him that defining the alibi was necessary, as much as I assured him that nothing out of what he had to say was to leave these walls, that no name, especially a woman's name, pronounced by him would be compromised—it was all in vain! He was ready to face any sad consequences of his stubbornness, but decidedly refused to answer the questions I needed answers for. I persisted because I sensed, with my nerves, with my entire nature, that the Frenchman was saying the truth and was innocent.

I was sure that this noble man was guided by the motives of chivalry and honor and not by fear or the desire to cover his criminal tracks.

2

But, alas! A chief detective cannot rely on his inner belief only; he cannot ignore precise facts, and that is why in that case I couldn't immediately give freedom back to the nice Frenchman, so, no matter whether I wanted or not, I handed him over to the investigating officer as I communicated my thoughts to the latter. The investigator turned out a stubborn, narrow-minded person, so he caught at the fact of concealing several hours that the Frenchman had spent in an unknown place the previous day and decided to arrest him. Thus the poor secretary was taken to prison.

Having handed this unpleasant case over to the investigator, I nevertheless ordered my functionary Mikhailov to figure out the conditions and the mode of everyday life of the princess's staff as far as it was possible. In a few days, Mikhailov found the following detail: About three months ago, the princess fired a footman, Pyotr Khodunov, who had been serving her for eight years and whom she trusted. This footman had traveled with the princess's staff several times, accompanying her abroad on her own comfortable yacht.

He was extremely disciplined, meek, and humble. The princess trusted him to such an extent that there were, according to her own testimony, cases when she would order Pyotr to open the secret fireproof safe and now bring some jewels from it, then return them.

He was fired for quite an odd reason: It turned out that this humble, sober man suddenly, with no apparent reason, started being rude, drinking heavily, and neglecting his job, as if he were deliberately fishing to be fired.

I thought it was strange.

Pyotr Khodunov was not on the staff list of the detective police. Just in case, I made inquiries to the Ministry of Justice concerning previous convictions, and how surprised I was when I found out that Pyotr Khodunov, such-and-such province, district, volost, and village, had been convicted twice for thefts and served terms of imprisonment for them.

I immediately rushed to search for him. It was not too hard, since the information bureau provided me with precise information about him.

But then doubts attacked me: I could arrest him—that wouldn't be a problem, but what would come out of it? He would, of

3

course, deny everything and say that it has been three whole months he hasn't worked for the princess, and anyway he would not give the stolen things back, but instead he would prefer to sit this out patiently, as fortunately he had been already trained at this in the past.

I preferred to put him under surveillance, authorizing two agents for that. For two days they watched him, reporting that Pyotr Khodunov led quite a disorderly life, sees many people, and drinks heavily in different taverns. Suddenly on the third day, the agents came running to me and embarrassedly confessed that they had "let slip" of Khodunov somewhere in Lefortovo. According to all the data, he had noticed the surveillance, neatly outwitted them, and … disappeared without a trace.

What could I do?

Having scolded my inept people, I immediately went to Khodunov's apartment intending to conduct a search and maybe arrest the latter as well. Although I didn't hope much for arresting him, since by the time we arrived at the apartment it had been about three hours after my agents had lost sight of Pete in Lefortovo, i.e., it was a period of time that was more than enough for the one smelling trouble to come back home, take the stolen things, and disappear without a trace.

Khodunov lived in an apartment with two rooms and a kitchen. He leased one of the rooms to a shoemaker, and in the other one he lived with a certain Tanya and her mother. Of course, we didn't find Pete there, but what I couldn't help noticing was the odd behavior of the women: They were not at all surprised at our arrival, as though they had been waiting for us, and I thought I even saw them exchange a mocking, triumphant look. They behaved rather defiantly. A thorough search didn't give any results. The women and the shoemaker as well were recklessly lying, as they kept affirming that it had been three days already since Pete had disappeared, while my people, as they had been maintaining surveillance, that same day saw Khodunov leaving his apartment. So I decided to arrest all three, escorting them to my office. I laid an ambush in case Pete should come back, although it was quite unlikely.

I immediately set to interrogations. The mother turned out to be a quite oppressed creature, slow-witted and illiterate, flatly denying everything. Her role was apparently passive. Since she as well turned out to be ill, suffering from a hemorrhage, I thought it possible to let her go home guarded by an agent. The daughter was different: nimble, pert, educated, and experienced. Just like her mother, she denied everything, and also quite well simulated indignation at the arrest, as she even promised to complain to somebody in another institution. I detained her at the police office. The shoemaker gave the same answers:

"I know nothing, there's nothing I know!"

But he quickly caved in; it took only for me to raise my voice at him:

"Ah, so you don't know?! Very well, you'll be inside right until we find Pete. And you'll serve your special time for harboring a thief, too."

"No wa-a-ay! Your Most Honorable Sir, I won't be inside because of some piece of—No, please let me go, and I'll tell you what I know."

"Where's Pete?"

"I don't know that. But it is true that an hour before you arrived at the apartment, Pete came rushing home like crazy, grabbed a little trunk, said goodbye to the broads, mentioned something about a dispatch to aunt Katya (this is the old lady's sister, I mean), and was gone."

"Where does this aunt Katya live?"

"Honestly, I don't know that."

"For how long have you been renting an apartment from Pete?"

"It's been more than two months now."

"Have you noticed any difference about their lifestyle within the past week?"

"Yeah, they had a poor life before, but lately they went on a spree. There are guests and drinking, and the grub's different now. The day before yesterday, they treated me to some good stuff, too. And then again, he gave those gold earrings to Tanya yesterday."

I let the shoemaker go and took him home in ambush.

It would be good to find this "aunt Katya," I thought.

Still, on the other hand, she wouldn't give Pete up either if she was interested in this affair. Anyway, I should have given it some thought.

The next day, it was reported that the mother asked for permission to send her arrested daughter some food and a change of underwear.

The food given to people in our police cells was good and plentiful, so the arrested, of course, were not in need for their own provisions, but I never objected such requests. The only thing I required was thorough preliminary examination of the parcels. This time, too, the only difference was that I wished to inspect Tanya's parcel by myself. It turned out rather modest: a pot of shchi, a round home-baked loaf, and a clean chemise.

Deep in thought, I was staring at the cut and pinched loaf when suddenly I had an idea.

I took a tiny piece of paper and scribbled small letters on one side: "Pete's dispatch received by aunt Katya. He asks what to do."

I ordered to bake this note and a pencil stub wet with saliva in a loaf made specially for this and give it to Tanya with her home basket, the shchi, and the chemise.

The next day, as Tanya was giving back the empty pot and the dirty chemise, my people found in the seam of its hem the sewn-in reply that she had written on my piece of paper. It was as follows: "Tell aunt Katya to send Pete a dispatch to Nizhny Novgorod (then the name of the street and the hotel) and write him that I am locked up."

In the evening, accompanied by two agents, I left on an express train to Nizhny.

I stayed in the Russia hotel, and I called the chief of the local detective department to come there. According to him, the place where Pete was staying was a lousy furnished accommodation somewhere across Oka. The advantage we had, though, was that the accommodation was held by an old man who served the detective police back in times and still had not torn his connections with it. He repeatedly did favors for the local chief, reporting on suspicious characters who visited his accommodation.

I decided to talk to him.

"Tell me, is Pyotr Khodunov staying at your place?"

"Sure, he's been renting a room for two days now."

"What does he do?"

"Devil knows! He leaves in the morning, he's gone for the whole day, and he comes back drunk from the fair toward evening."

"Listen! You were in the detective business yourself before, so you see, you can help us."

"With greatest pleasure!" the old man replied, livening up like an old warhorse hearing a familiar signal.

"Tell me, is there an available room next to Khodunov?"

"One became available just today."

"Great! My people will take it. What about the walls between them—are they thick?"

"You're kidding me! I could say those are plank partitions."

"Khodunov is not home now, is he?"

"No, he left in the morning, and he won't probably be back till the night."

"Wonderful! Here's what you should do, my friend: Now go and drill a couple of holes through the wall and disguise them well—hammer some nails in next to them or something, and I will send two 'guests' to you."

"At your orders …."

In an hour two out-of-towners, looking like merchants with suitcases in their hands, haggled a little bit and occupied the room next to Khodunov's. Through the drilled holes, they viewed Pete's room, and in the evening they saw him come back, tipsy, get undressed quickly, take two bundles out of his pockets—one small, one bigger—and, having hidden them under the pillow, tumble into bed.

The next morning one of the agents reported to me on the phone to the Russian hotel:

"Pete got up, washed himself, then took something from under the pillow, hid one of the bundles in the pocket of his jacket, and the other one, a small one, he carefully unwrapped, turned to the window, took its contents out with two fingers, and squinted at it in the light. A pink stone sparkled in his fingers. After that Pete complacently smiled, wrapped the stone in a piece of paper again and hid it in the bottom right pocket of his vest. Then he sat down in a hurry and wrote a letter and sealed the envelope, and now he seems to be about to leave."

"Do not take your eyes from him even for a minute and pass this order of mine to the agents of the outdoor guard. Remember, you are personally responsible for exact execution of this order."

I immediately rushed to the other bank of Oka, and on my way I met my subordinates keeping their eyes on some character walking ahead them.

Joining them inconspicuously, I started following Pete.

The latter was walking fast and led us to the fair building that was occupied by the post office during the fair. Khodunov entered it. Together with us, around ten people of the local agents walked in. Pete came up to a small window, bought a stamp, stuck it on, and went toward the box to drop the letter. At this same moment I came up to him and cried for the entire post office to hear:

"Freeze! I am the chief of Moscow detective police. Give me the diamond!"

Pete got confused, opened his mouth wide, and finally muttered:

"What do you want? What diamond?"

"The one that's in the right pocket of your vest!" saying this, I dipped my fingers into his vest, quickly released the stone from the piece of paper, and raised it high overhead. Sparkling in my fingers was a pale-pink stone, the color of a delicate rosy dawn. An astonished humming of voices went across the stupefied post office. Pete was completely lost.

"My god! How on earth did you know that? That's unbelievable! Well, take the pearls, too, since it's impossible to hide things from you! It's like you're seeing through! What a deal! What a trick!"

"Where's the carnelian ring?"

"I don't have it, sir, I just don't have it!"

"What did you do with it?"

"I sold it yesterday, here at the fair, to a Persian. It doesn't cost anything, I only got five rubles for it ...."

"Bring us to the Persian right now!"

The Persian's shop was shown to us, and the ring was taken from him.

Therefore the thief was arrested, and all the things were found. In the evening, Pete was sent to Moscow under escort, and I was so glad I decided to celebrate the success with two subordinates from Moscow. Thus we went to the fair's café *chantant* in the evening.

Only a Russian of the pre-revolutionary epoch can have an idea of what Nizhny's *chantant* was like in the period of a fair. The drunken merchants' Russian boundless large way of doing things, nourished and inspired by the fantastic gains made in the recent couple of days, windfall money, and the energy that had been accumulated for a year and then will be spent in a short period of time—here are the environment and the atmosphere that I went to. Somehow my presence in the restaurant became known, and we had barely had time to occupy a table near the stage and knock back a glass of Monopole Sec each, when I started noticing that necks and heads would stretch toward us, not only from the tables near us, but from the tables in the distance as well. First people would glance at us every now and then with careful curiosity. As the bottles were emptied, though, shyness was disappearing, and people smiled at us, winked, raised their glasses, and drank to our health, or even pointed sometimes. Finally, some merchant, who had had quite a few, burst into the hall with a glass in his hands and pronounced in a thick, although thundering voice, addressing to everyone in general and no-one in particular:

"Orthodox Christians! Are you aware of who is among us? You're not? I will tell you …. My fellow-townsman, we're both from Moscow, Mister Koshkov! There are awesome sturgeons you can find in the White-Stone[1]! He and I are not like your Nizhny's small fry! I guess you've heard that today in the post office he came up to that cheat and said right away, 'Take your boot off! There's a green diamond hidden in between your toes!' So, what do you think? It really was! We should be pleasing this man. He is protecting our capitals from all kinds of scum and provides us great benefits!"

The drunk Muscovite's words were a signal: I was immediately surrounded by people, some shaking my hands, some trying to kiss me. One especially expansive and just as drunk subject turned out his huge wallet and shouted:

"You need money, perhaps? Take it without ceremonies, my dear friend! Take as much as you need …."

Another one brought the orchestra to the hall playing a flourish. People cried 'Hooray!'

The cabaret singers from all over Europe were showered with 100-rubles bills, and a lavish party started—irrepressible and wild, boundless in expenses or extravagances—in short, a party of a scope that cannot be known, and even the idea of which cannot be familiar to anyone who wasn't born with a Russian soul.

I returned to my hotel stunned, touched, and completely exhausted.

Next morning I left Nizhny and went back to Moscow.

Having summoned Tanya, I said to her:

---

[1] The White-Stone (Russian: Белокаменная, *be-lah-káh-men-nah-ya*) is a literary epithet for Moscow.

"Well, stop clowning! Tell me, where is Pete?"

"Oh, why would you, sir, keep asking the same stuff all the time? I told you many times already that I know nothing about him."

"So there's really nothing you know, huh?"

"May God strike me! May I drop dead! May my eyes burst! I know nothing!"

"So you don't even spare your eyes, do you?"

"I don't, sir, may they burst if I am lying!"

I slowly took the diamond out of my pocket, unwrapped the paper, and showed it to her from a distance.

"Do you see that?"

Tanya blushed and whispered, "I do."

I took out my little note with her writing on the back side of it.

"And do you see that?"

"I wrote it," Tanya whispered, barely audibly.

"There you go! And you're saying 'May my eyes burst!' It was I who sent you the note, and it was I who ripped your reply from the chemise!"

Ah, Tanya, Tanya! It was you yourself who gave up your precious Pete!

Tanya went off into downright hysterics.

Giving the stolen things back to the princess Shakhovsky-Glebov-Streshnev, I noticed not only her joy, but considerable confusion as well.

"My God, how horrible that is! I distrusted this most honest and absolutely innocent man! How can I look in his eyes after that?"

It is unknown to me how the princess managed to look into the eyes of the faithful Frenchman. But the image of this chivalrous man was imprinted in my memory for a long time afterwards.

Vasya Smyslov

The detective police of Moscow knew Vasya Smyslov very well.

We repeatedly arrested him for petty larcenies; however, every time he completed serving his imprisonment sentence, he continued with his "craft."

Once, about two days after a rather significant burglary in one of apartments on Povarskaya St.—a burglary that had not yet been solved—my official phone suddenly rang. I answered:

"Hello? Who is it?"

"Is that you, Mister Chief?"

"It's me."

"I wish you good health; it's Vasya Smyslov speaking."

"Hello, Vasya! What's that you have to say?"

"It's that your fools let me slip again the day before yesterday!"

"Really? Nonsense!"

"I'm telling you! 'Cause it was my work down on Povarskaya."

"Well, what can I say? You're lucky, Vasya, but watch out, take care not to get caught, though!"

"No way, Mister Chief, we got the hang now, we won't be caught, you gotta be kidding!"

"Oh, Vasya, you really shouldn't be bragging about it!"

"Have no doubt, you won't catch me!"

And Vasya hung up.

Smyslov was a cheerful fellow, not without cunning, and, as odd as it may sound, quite good-natured. He apparently was not devoid of sense of humor, so, as he sensed the funny side of my situation, after that day he started calling me every time after a successful larceny. When he neatly filched a number of watches from one of the jewelry shops on Kuznetsky by pushing out the glass in a shop window, Vasya called me on the phone:

"It's me again, Mister Chief! So, is it a nice job on Kuznetsky?"

"What can I say, good job! Not a single weak spot in it …."

"There you go! And you keep telling me you'll catch me— well, that will never happen!"

"We'll have to see about it, Vasya!"

"There's nothing to see. I'm telling you, you won't catch me."

After a pause, Vasya went on:

"Here's what I have to tell you, Mister Koshkin: I am preparing a bigger affair over here, so when I'm done, I'll call you without fail."

"Oh, Vasya, you'd better not—you're teasing me!"

Vasya laughed with pleasure into the receiver:

"That's okay, Mister Chief, just be patient, that'll be useful for you!"

And Vasya rang off.

The stupid situation started vexing me. I was sure Vasya would keep his word, so I decided to take measures.

I made the following order: In the future, as soon as I signaled the duty room with three long calls, the functionary on duty mast immediately dash to one of the free telephones and ask the central station about the telephone number that is currently connected to the chief of the detective police. At the same time, another functionary was obliged to open the police sequential recorder of telephone numbers that indicated the address of every number. The third functionary, with two agents would need to be getting dressed in the meantime, and, as he received the address from the first two, to take the standby vehicle and rush to the indicated location.

We had been waiting for Vasya's call for two days. Finally, on the third day someone called me, and when I came up to the phone, I heard Vasya's voice. Holding the receiver in my right hand, with my left hand I pressed the electric button on my desk and made the signal to set off our plan.

Now my entire task boiled down to keeping Vasya on the phone for a certain time by a conversation that would be interesting enough to him, but not to arouse his suspicion.

Vasya started the way he always did:

"I promised to call you, Mister Chief, so here I go."

"Tell me, Vasya, how come you're not afraid to call me? What if I find out where you're calling from and reveal your place of residence by the phone number?"

Vasya expressively whistled.

"You're messing with the wrong person. What am I, a fool, to call you from my family's or my friends' place? Thank God, there are phones in Moscow on every corner, and mother Moscow is pretty big. So go search for me!"

"So I guess you're a brainy fellow, Vasya!"

"That's okay, God gave us a brain. And last night we worked again a little bit on Myasnitskaya. You've heard, I guess? It's only too bad we took so little!"

"So that's what you're bragging about, huh? Bid deal! Have you heard what happened at the same time last night on Tverskaya?"

"No, I haven't. What happened, Mister Chief?" There was curiosity in Vasya's voice.

"There you go, Vasya, squandering your talents on trifles, so that you don't even get to know the real stuff!"

"So what happened? Tell me!"

"What happened was that a jewelry shop on Tverskaya was cleaned out."

"You serious?"

"You bet I am."

"How much did they take, Mister Chief?"

"Well, I heard around three hundred grand."

"Damn …." Some envy appeared in Vasya's voice.

"So what do you think, Vasya? Whose doing can it be?"

Vasya thought for a while and then said:

"None other than Crooked Seryozha."

"Who's Crooked Seryozha?"

"Don't you know? The one who gangs up with Pocked Tanya."

"I know Pocked Tanya."

"So here you go—they're at work together."

"How long has it been since you saw Crooked Seryozha?"

"It's been a week at least, I guess."

"Listen, Vasya, why don't you help me find out where Seryozha is now? As a thank you, when you're caught, I won't forget your favor and will as all kinds of leniency for you."

"Really, maybe I should look for him," Vasya said pensively, but then added: "But anyway, I won't find 'im!"

"Why not?"

"'Cause you, Mister Chief, just told me it was three hundred grand, so would he stay in Moscow with this lot of money? I guess the bird is long flown!"

Vasya wanted to add something else, but he suddenly gave a cry, the receiver started crackling into my ear, and I realized that Vasya was caught.

In a quarter of an hour, he was already in my office.

"So, Vasya, who wins? Who outwitted whom?"

"Good job, I am gonna have to say, Mister Chief!"

Vasya scratched the back of his head, hesitated a little, and then said unconfidently:

"May I ask you about those 300 grand: Were you just saying that, for the trickery?"

"Sure I was. I needed to keep you on the phone with an interesting conversation."

Vasya admiringly rolled up his eyes to the ceiling, hit himself in the chest with the fist, and pronounced emotionally:

"What a sly dog you are, Mister Koshkin!!"

A Tough Errand

It happened in Riga in the early 90s, i.e., when I was the head of the Riga Detective Department.

A large diamond was stolen from an icon of the Mother of God at a local cathedral. All the circumstances of the case indicated that the larceny was carried out by the church's watchman, who lived in the cathedral's basement. Although the search conducted in his place didn't produce any positive results, some inquiries I made concerning his past confirmed my suspicions, since it turned out that the watchman had been convicted once for larceny and had served a term of imprisonment for it.

Having this information, I decided to arrest him.

He spent about five days in a police cell, during which I interrogated him three times. No matter how hard I tried to catch him in contradictions, though, I couldn't—he would simply fall silent, unwilling to answer my questions.

I then tried to switch to his wife, but the woman turned out to be sly and rude, but not too talkative. Not only would she plead complete unawareness, but as well she asserted that her husband had been arrested illegally and in vain.

After these interrogations, I only acquired stronger faith in the guilt of both of them, but what was I to do? How could I prove it? How could I find the diamond? Suddenly I had an idea!

I remembered that in the watchman's room there was a big double bed, and I decided to use it. I summoned two agents and explained my plan to them: The next day, following my call, the watchman's wife would come for interrogation at 12 o'clock; I would hold her for an hour, and in her absence the agents would need to sneak into the watchman's dwelling. One of them (Pankratiev) would get under the bed and bury himself under miscellaneous junk and rags that I had noticed during my search, and he would have to stay there until 8 o'clock in the evening—i.e., until I come. The other one would use a picklock to return the locks to their initial state and would then leave.

No sooner said than done.

The next day I thoroughly interrogated the watchman's wife, and as I achieved nothing, I said with false disappointment:

"Devil knows you both! Maybe you really are innocent! All right, I will release your husband today, but remember that both of you are under my suspicion."

An hour after I let go of the watchman's wife, I released the husband, too, announcing to him that I was releasing him in accordance with the law, but in my heart I believed he was guilty.

At 8 o'clock, I came to the cathedral with agents and knocked on the watchman's room's door. When they saw us, they started dashing around in panic. I loudly shouted:

"Pankratiev, where's the diamond?"

Suddenly, to their indescribable horror, something started moving under the bed, and disheveled Pankratiev, crawling from beneath it, cheerfully roared:

"In the firewood, sir!"

Dead silence fell.

"You heard that?" I said to the watchman. "Now give me the diamond!"

"He's lying, Your Most Honorable Sir! I know nothing."

"Well, Pankratiev, tell me how it was."

"There's not much to tell, sir. I got under the bed, lay there for about an hour, and then the woman came, and then the man in a couple of hours.

"They fired up the samovar, sat at the table to have tea, had it, and then the woman said:

'You better go check, Dmitrich[2], is it okay in the firewood?'

'Where would it go?' he replied.

"However, the man went outside and brought a log in a while. They picked at it, looked inside, and it was there. So the wife said:

'You better leave it in the room—that's the best way.'

And he replied:

'No. You never know when they could come again. I better take it back to its place.'

"And he did. When he came back, he and his wife first started to make fun of you, and what happened next, I don't even want to tell, sir. These bastards scratched almost all over my face with this spring mattress."

"So, what do you say after this?" I ask the watchman again.

"They dreamed about all this! I don't know anything, there's nothing I know, and I never said bad stuff about you."

We had nothing left to do but search through the stacks of firewood that were piled up by the back wall of the cathedral. On a hot trail, we detected where the spot approximately was, then looked through and chopped about a hundred and fifty logs, and we finally found the precious stone.

"Sir," Pankratiev told me, "for God's sake, please do not make me go on errands like this again, 'cause I almost died: I was lying under this bed for eight hours, and I was wrapped up in this dirty, stinking underwear and rags. That's too much for me! Ptooey!" and he juicily spat.

---

[2] Dmitrich is the shortened patronymic for the name Dmitry.

A Commercial Enterprise

In 1908 or 1909 I received a notification from the Headquarters of the Post and Telegraph Offices stating that in recent months many towns of Russia had been flooded with artificially rubbed-off postage stamps with the values of 7 and 10 kopecks. The rubbing was so perfect that one could detect it only with a strong magnifying glass. There were grounds to suppose that this fraud was the work of a well-organized gang that had cast its nets pretty much over all of Russia. The rumor had it that the organization's center was in Warsaw.

Having this information, I ordered agents to inspect in their districts all the tobacco shops, sundries shops, and other shops, in which, following the ancient tradition, stamps were sold.

Moscow is big, so this operation took quite a long time.

Meanwhile, I noticed that recently in newspapers many announcements appeared from collectors who offered to buy old stamps. So I decided to conduct searches at collectors' houses, and I must admit that those searches resulted in nothing except for huge stocks of old stamps.

My agents, equipped with magnifying glasses that had been obtained specially for them, found stamps that they thought were suspicious in many tobacco and sundries shops, took them, and brought them to me. I began to examine them thoroughly.

The rubbing was perfect: not only were there no slightest traces of old postmarks, but the teeth on the edges were completely intact as well, and the glue was preserved, etc. The only thing one could notice comparing two stamps, a new one and a rubbed-off one, was that the ink on the latter was somewhat paler and looked a little faded. The difference was so slight that I had to send a batch of those stamps to the Central Post Office for expert examination, and it was only there where their unfitness was ascertained. For some reason, there were only separate pieces of such stamps found, and never whole sheets. The shopkeepers/salesmen, when interrogated, in unison claimed that they had acquired the stamps in post departments and had no idea those were bad. There was only one of them, apparently an extremely timid person frightened by the involvement of authorities, who frankly confessed that he had gotten the stocks of stamps for his shop from a well-known stamp collector who lived in one of the Kozitsky Lanes, a certain E. He would receive them from E. at a discount of 1 kopeck each.

I sent two agents on a mission to E. During the search, no rubbed-off stamps were found at his place, but one thing drew the attention of my assistant V.E.Andreev, who headed the search, and it was the fact that in E's wallet a delivery note was found for an item from Warsaw, and the item named in it was rather extravagant: a sack of feathers! Why would a stamp collector need to order feathers from Warsaw? As though there are not enough geese, ducks and other birds in Moscow. This E. was arrested and taken to the detective police station. At first he denied his guilt, but after two days in a cell, when he was brought to a face-to-face interrogation with the tobacco shopkeeper who had previously given E's name and now recognized him, he gave up, confessing to everything, and he vastly helped us in solving this entire criminal machination.

He told us the following: about three months earlier, some person came to him, a Jew by appearance, sold him a few specimens of rather rare stamps, talked a lot on various subjects, and ended the conversation with an advantageous offer: to supply E. with a batch of neatly rubbed-off 7- and 10-kopecks stamps at a discount of three kopecks off each.

He at once showed his sample. "After a lot of hesitation I yielded to temptation and expressed my consent to the fraud. Then my tempter gave me the name of Zilberstein, to whom I was supposed to write to Warsaw to be called for. We exchanged letters, and since then from time to time I receive from Zilberstein batches of stamps packed in sacks with feathers so that the stamps cannot be felt."

"Do you think," I asked, "the last delivery note's sack has already been delivered?"

"Judging by the time, it must have been."

I sent a man with the delivery note to the goods station, and the sack was shortly brought to our office. We poured the feathers out, and among them we found up to 10 thousand stamps. They were laid in small packages of 100 stamps, and each of those was carefully tied up with a blue thread.

It would not have been difficult, of course, to write to Zilberstein a letter signed by E. with the next order and arrest him in Warsaw, in the post office, at the moment he would receive correspondence to be called for; however, the stamps enterprise had spread all over Russia, so the case required revealing the origin of production and terminating it completely. Meanwhile, Zilberstein might have turned out merely an intermediary, not the organization's worker or its head.

These were the grounds that made me refuse the idea of immediately arresting Zilberstein, so I began to invent a reason to go to Warsaw. I was assisted in that by that same arrested collector.

"That's easy!" he said. "Zilberstein repeatedly invited me in his letters to come to Warsaw to discuss some new and rather profitable affair. I suspect, based on his hints that it is about distributing rubbed-off revenue stamps."

"Zilberstein hasn't ever seen you, has he?"

"No."

"Great! Make a pause of about three days, and then write to him saying that you're ready to come to Warsaw for negotiations and you thus ask him to choose the exact place of your future meeting."

E. agreed to satisfy my demand, but he said:

"You see, sir, that not only have I repented of my crime, but I am also ready to contribute to solving this case by all means. Please, release me, I miss my home so badly!"

I was in a difficult situation, so I decided to consult the court prosecutor, Arnoldi.

"I don't know what I should advise you," he told me. "If you release E., he may run away or ruin the entire case for you. Still, do as you want, Arkady Frantsevich. You're the doctor."

"I will grant you a pretrial release," I said to E., "but I will appoint two agents to look after you, and they will be watching you day and night."

"For goodness' sake! Why all these precautions?"

"Well, pardon me, but they are necessary."

"All right, well, let it be!"

In about three days, E. wrote to Zilberstein a letter to be called for. In this letter he expressed his consent to negotiating the profitable affair, but explained that he couldn't come himself, but was ready to send his brother instead, whom he trusted as he trusted himself. Soon Zilberstein's reply came with details of the day, hour, and place of meeting.

For this meeting Zilberstein chose the Saxon Garden and a bench right opposite to the summer theater entrance. For identification, he asked Mr. E. to hold the local Russian newspaper *Varshavsky Dnevnik* in his hands. E. immediately wrote back saying that the time and the place were acceptable, and I started preparing for the trip. By the appointed time, I left for Warsaw with two agents.

At the agreed hour, I was in the Saxon Garden on the indicated bench and was attentively reading *Varshavsky Dnevnik*. There was no one around me, except for a fat Jewish woman with a baby, sitting opposite me. Half an hour later, no one had yet shown up. An hour later, still no one had shown up. I was about to leave regretfully, thinking that something absolutely unforeseen must have delayed or frightened Zilberstein. Suddenly that same Jewish woman crossed the courtyard and sat next to me. After keeping silence for a little while, she bewitchingly smiled and asked me:

"Tell me, monsieur, are you Russian?"

"I am."

"Ooh! I like Russians, those are good, generous people!"

I bowed.

"Do you live in Warsaw or are you a visitor?"

"A visitor, ma'am."

"I thought so! You do not look like a Varsovian. Are you from St. Petersburg?"

"No, I am from Moscow."

"From Moscow?!" she smiled as if surprised, then quickly leaned toward my ear, and whispered, "Well, then now I will show you Mr. Zilberstein at last!"

She led me to Trembacki St., brought me closer to a small café, and pointed at the table right by the mirror window.

There was a Jew of around 40, ginger, quite decently dressed, sitting at it.

He looked at us through the window and smiled to my guide.

I entered the café and went toward Zilberstein. He rose to greet me, and we shook hands in silence. We sat down.

"It is really nice to meet such a good man! We worked so well together, and you always paid so punctually. I mean, doing geschäft with you is real pleasure!"

I smiled.

"Well, as a matter of fact, it wasn't me who you worked with, but my brother. But it doesn't matter, of course."

"Right, so what's the difference? Your brother wrote to us that it was you who was coming, so I very well know that you are not Mr. E., but his brother. Does it really matter at all?"

"I should say though that my last name is E., too, but, of course, I am only the brother of your customer," and for more credibility I took out my passport and opened it before Zilberstein.

"Why would I need your passport? Is it like I do not see right away who I am dealing with here?" However, he dipped his eyes into the document. "You know, Mr. E., before we talk business, how about we have a glass or two? Well?"

"It would be nice to have breakfast first—I am hungry."

"We can have breakfast, too! Why not?"

"Yes, but it's not too cozy here! Shall we go to some cleaner restaurant?"

"It shows, Mr. E., that you are a true aristocrat. Doing it in a big way, if I may say!" Zilberstein looked at me admiringly.

"Right. Thank God, I cannot complain, I'm having good turnovers!"

"Well, do you know what I am going to tell you? If we have a deal, you'll be a millionaire! Believe the word of Yankel Zilberstein!"

"All right, all right! Let's discuss it later, Mr. Zilberstein, and now it would be great to eat!"

"Let's go, let's go, Mr. E. I know one restaurant not far from here. I know you will like: they serve flake, and zrazy, and comber[3] that are so good that even Mr. Rothschild wouldn't say no to them!"

Zilberstein brought me to a quite nice restaurant.

We had three shots of Starka[4] each or so, and the Jew softened.

"What a pleasant and sociable person you are! It is so nice to deal with you!" he would exclaim every minute.

We started the breakfast.

---

[3] Polish traditional dishes. Flaki is a tripe soup; zrazy are meat roulades; and comber (pronounced *tsom-ber*) is roast wild boar's back served with hawthorn sauce.

[4] Starka is a kind of dry vodka.

"You know, Mr. E., I want to propose you such a thing that if up until now we have been earning kopecks, with the new geschäft we'll be earning rubles!"

"Right, you gave me a hint in one of your letters. I am not sure, but it seemed to me you meant revenue stamps?"

"Yiddishe Kopf[5]!" Zilberstein exclaimed admiringly. "Yes, this is exactly what I was giving a hint about. Just think of the difference. Five-rubles, ten-rubles, and, finally, my God, forty-ruble stamps! Do you understand?"

"I understand very well. But before we discuss it, I need to take a look at the goods."

"He-he, of course you do! Who would buy goods sight unseen? Especially such delicate ones."

"This is exactly what I am talking about. Show me a sample, or maybe the production site, too, so that I could evaluate the quality, as well as reliability and scope of this business."

"For how long are you planning to stay in Warsaw?"

"For a few days at least, depending on how long the affair requires me to stay."

"Well, then there's no need to hurry! I will talk to my companion, and tomorrow we will show you both samples and, if only he agrees, the manufacturer. I am ready to bring you there even now, but I have to coordinate my actions with him, and he is distrustful and timorous."

However, after the second bottle of wine, Zilberstein became imbued with ardent love toward me, and he pompously exclaimed:

"Well, why would I be tormenting you—here are the samples!"

---

[5] 'Yiddishe Kopf' is transliteration from the Yiddish phrase meaning 'Jewish head,' which is usually an exclamation of surprise at someone's intelligence or slyness.

And he took several revenue stamps out of his wallet. I began to scrutinize this amazing work.

Tipsy, Zilberstein reproachfully exclaimed:

"What are you doing? Do you think you will see something with your naked eye?! Please take the magnifier, Mr. E., take the magnifier, here you go!" he held a magnifying glass out to me.

"Thank you, I have a magnifying glass. I first want to get a general impression."

Having looked at the stamps from every side, I started to examine them with the magnifying glass as well. Finally, after I finished with this, I imposingly pronounced:

"The goods are good, flawless—what can I say? It's even surprising!"

Zilberstein smiled complacently.

"Maybe you think that Zilberstein is bragging and showing you real stamps?"

"No, I don't think that. But, of course, to make a large order I need to have a solid faith in the technical setting. Because one cannot examine every single stamp, right? Maybe, Mr. Zilberstein, you will talk to your companion and arrange it somehow?"

"All right, Mr. E. Tomorrow at two in the afternoon, be at Prague: There, on such-and-such street, in the house No. 43, there is a small restaurant, although somewhat dirty and mostly visited by furmans[6], but it is reliable in every way. I will introduce you to my companion, and maybe he will agree to show you something."

We settled on that, and I called a footman and asked for the check.

"We will pay the German way," Zilberstein said to me. "I will pay for what I ate, and you will pay for what you ate."

---

[6] Furman is 'cabman' in Yiddish.

"Well, why should we engage in such calculations? For such a pleasant acquaintance, I will pay for everything."

"Why would you?" Zilberstein protested lightly. "Why don't we do it the German way?"

"That's all right! Tomorrow you will pay, and that will be the German way."

We went out. Zilberstein shook my hand for a long time, declaring his love and praising my generosity, but finally we parted, and I went to my room in the hotel.

After spending two hours in it, I left in the evening and in the twilight went to the local detective police. I spoke to Mr. Kowalik, the head of the Warsaw department. After briefly telling him the events, I asked him to give me two agents for tomorrow dressed as furmans (cabmen) for surveillance over Zilberstein and his accomplice. I added the two agents that I brought from Moscow to the two Warsaw agents.

The next day, at one o'clock precisely, I was entering a slightly dirty restaurant in Prague, where at the counter there was already a crowd of people of utterly proletarian in appearance. Soon one of the cabmen agents joined them. As soon as I sat at the table in the next, "clean" room, Zilberstein and his companion came in. Zilberstein joyfully greeted me and introduced me to his companion, saying his name was Grynszpan. We ordered some food.

Grynszpan was strikingly different from Zilberstein. The former turned out as cautious and secretive as the latter was trustful and expansive. Several times during the breakfast, Grynszpan stopped and interrupted Zilberstein. It happened when Zilberstein, under an impulse of praising his goods, snatched at his wallet, intending to take new samples out of it. It again happened when Zilberstein, carried away by the size of future gains, confessed that the scope of their work had spread all over Russia.

After talking for about an hour, I generally expressed my consent to take wide participation in dealing in revenue stamps in Moscow, but the condition was that I needed to be familiarized with the production technology.

Cautious Grynszpan did not give me the final answer, but asked me to come to the same restaurant tomorrow, and he promised to announce his decision then. Obviously, he was intending to make inquiries concerning me in the hotel within the following twenty-four hours, or maybe even watch me and my walks around Warsaw.

We came out of the restaurant, and we were long time saying goodbye to each other at the entrance. But when I finally was sure that my people and both cabmen were there, I parted with the swindlers and headed to my place. As I was concerned about being watched by the cautious Grynszpan and afraid to disrupt the case, I decided not to leave the hotel any more that day. Late at night, one of my agents stopped by my room and reported that they had been attentively watching both characters the whole day, and they were certain that the two lived on the outskirts of Prague at a bookbinder's shop with a sign reading "Y. Grynszpan's Bookbinder's Shop." During the day, several times they left and came back, and finally one of them, the shorter one (Zilberstein) came back for the last time at 9 o'clock, and after that they closed the shop, and the light was turned on in the windows on the side of it.

On the same evening, I received an urgent telegram from my assistant in Moscow that informed me of a bloody murder and burglary in one of the apartments of Povarskoy Lane, so as I was in a hurry to come back, I decided to speed the things up and conduct a search immediately in the bookbinder's shop without waiting for next day's meeting. Besides, everything seemed to indicate that the production of stamps was organized at that place exactly: Both accomplices lived together and used the sign of a bookbinder's shop as a cover, and it is a good deception, since such craft requires paper and glue and all kinds of instruments for embossing that possibly fit for rubbing off and cutting out stamps.

I called Kowalik and informed him of my decision to conduct a search immediately. He expressed the desire to take part in it, so we, with his and my agents, went to Prague. We knocked on the bookbinder's shop's door and didn't receive an answer for a long time. So we started hammering on the door harder, and, finally, we heard a frightened male voice behind it:

"Who is it?"

"Police, open up!"

"Oy vey! What police? What do you want, Mr. Oberpolizeimeister?"

"Open up this instant, or we will break the door open!"

The threat worked, and Zilberstein, in slippers and shaking with fear, opened the door. We rapidly went in the room—the shop.

There was a counter, a workbench, a table, and two stools. Standing aside was a bed, from which toward us a disheveled Grynszpan was rising. The next room was the dining room, and farther on was the room of Mr. and Mrs. Zilberstein, or, to be more exact, Mr. and Mrs. Grynszpan, because Zilberstein turned out to be Grynszpan's brother, who had appropriated another last name and used it as a cover when receiving correspondence to be called for. When we arrived—me, especially—the first words of Grynszpan addressed to Zilberstein were:

"So, Yasha? Didn't I tell you?!"

We set to the search, but, to my anxiety, we found absolutely nothing in the shop or in the dining room. There was the third room left, the married couple's bedroom, and some howls, moans, and groans sounded from it.

"Gentlemen police, please do not enter there! My sick wife is in there," Zilberstein addressed to us.

"Impossible! We have to look through the entire house," was the reply.

"But please, be quicker and quieter!"

"All right, all right, don't worry!"

We entered the bedroom. A fat Jewish woman was writhing on the bed, deafening the room with her cries.

"What's with her?" I asked Zilberstein.

"The thing that happens to women."

"Which one?"

"Madam Zilberstein is 'expecting.'"

"What is she expecting?"

"Little Gershe or baby Sarah!"

"Oh, so tha-a-at's what it is!"

But Madam Zilberstein's writhing seemed unnatural to me, and her already exaggerated howls were gradually increasing as we approached her bed.

"Ooh, ooh! Don't touch me! Drop dead, Yankel! My torments are your fault. Oh! Ooh!"

She was clearly overdoing it, so I offered to send for a midwife attached to the police.

"Why would you bother?!" Zilberstein became nervous. "There is a midwife living right near us, so we can call for her."

"No, we better have ours come."

"Ooh! But it will take so long, and the local one would come right away!"

"That's all right, you'll wait! We'll take a cabman and get her here in no time."

The search was going on, and one of the agents went to bring the police midwife.

I thought the features of the moaning Jewish woman were familiar.

I looked closer, and—oh! I recognized my yesterday's acquaintance from the Saxon Garden. Without showing it, I asked Zilberstein:

"How long has your wife been suffering like this?"

"Ooh! It's been two weeks she hasn't risen from this bed. Contractions come all the time, now abate for a minute, now come back again! She is suffering very, very much!"

The woman, as she heard my questions and her husband's answer, started to howl even louder. Then she turned her head to me and pronounced in a dying voice:

"You know, I sometimes ask God for death, that's how shvakh[7] I feel at times. Ooh, ooh! Here it comes again! Ooh!"

"Yes, Mrs. Zilberstein, today you feel much worse than yesterday in the Saxon Garden," I said calmly.

Mrs. Zilberstein stopped moaning at once, quickly turned her head to me and fixed her Syrian eyes on me.

"So, what do you mean by that? Well, yes. Today it's worse, and yesterday it was better. Just like now, I feel better, much better! I think I will even get up," and Mrs. Zilberstein put her fat feet down on the floor from the bed.

When the agent came back with the midwife, she flatly refused a medical examination, threw a housecoat on her shoulders, and stepped aside.

We thoroughly examined and felt the entire bed, but ... found absolutely nothing. Tapping the walls, especially the one that the bed was moved close to, wasn't any more successful.

Suddenly one of the agents who was conducting the search in this room claimed that the floor boards, on the exact spot where the bed was, somehow shook when pressed. They were lifted, and underneath them there was a ladder leading to the basement. We brought candles and descended downstairs. There was a small corridor, more of a trench, about 15 feet long, and in the end of it was a small room of around 200 square feet. This "catacomb" turned out to be the place of the stamps' "rejuvenation." We found two sleeping workers in it.

In one of the corners was a special boiler, where the old stamps were boiled and steamed off. In the middle of the room was a table with drawing boards, where the stamps were to be dried and smeared with glue again.

---

[7] Shvakh is transliteration of the Yiddish word meaning "bad."

But what was the most interesting is that we found several thousands of stamps in whole sheets. There was one sheet in progress lying there, an unfinished one, and by examining it we had an opportunity to reconstruct the method of its manufacture. Apparently they took cleaned and yet still a little moist stamps and placed them on the drawing board, glue side down, ten and twenty stamps on each side, depending on the desired size of the square.

The stamps were put together with extreme care, so that the teeth of one stamp entered the gaps between the teeth of the next one, and thus a sort of a continuous material would come out.

After that they took a very narrow (a millimeter-wide or maybe even narrower) ribbon of thinnest cigarette paper of the same length as the entire sheet and glued it along the matching teeth between the rows of the stamps. Then they took a special instrument (that was right there on the table, too) that resembled a little wheel for cutting raw dough. Its difference from the utensil was that sticking out on the edges of this wheel (perpendicular to its circumference) were close and sharp little needles. If you held this instrument by the handle and rolled the wheel along the glued space between the stamps, holes would be made in it again, but the rows of stamps would remain tightly connected to each other, thanks to the cigarette paper, and one would probably need a microscope to detect this truly filigree work.

The brothers Grynszpan had nothing left to do but confess.

Saving their own skin, they spat it all out. Within the six months of their work, they had managed to cast a wide net all over Russia. In each large city there were their agents who recruited distributors, and "collectors" who supplied them with old stamps. The organization was so populous that appearing before Warsaw Judicial Court, where this case was heard, were several hundreds of the accused. What the smart "entrepreneurs" were sentenced to, I do not remember. Still, I remember that I had a feeling of deep satisfaction that time when leaving Warsaw and coming back to Moscow, where life was still going on and kept on bringing up new anti-heroes.

The Gilevich Case

Many years of work experience made me develop a habit to patiently hear out everyone who wished to talk to the chief of police personally. Although those conversations took a lot of time, and although I was bothered with trifles a lot, not only did I always hear everyone out, but I also took notes on everything I thought was worthy of the slightest attention.

I put those notes in a special drawer, and I took them from there as needed. The need came up more frequently than a reader may suppose. As boundless and diverse as the criminal world is, it still has its laws, tricks, rituals, skills, and, if you will, traditions. Criminal elements are connected by a more or less common psychology, and in order to successfully struggle against them, it is quite useful to note bright and unusual things about them that impress you. In short, the brief notes and records I was collecting repeatedly stood me in good stead.

This was vividly demonstrated in the Gilevich case.

It started like this.

"Sir, there is a student who wishes to see you, but, if I may report, he is quite drunk," the inspector on duty reported to me in my office in Moscow, on Malyi Gnezdikovsky Lane.

"Okay. Let him in ...."

In a minute the student entered the room. Hesitantly, he came up to the desk and immediately gripped the back of a leather armchair. He was a sturdy fellow with a red face and disheveled hair, wearing a somewhat tattered student uniform. He stared at me with his turbid eyes and drunkenly smiled.

"How can I help you?" I asked.

"Excuse me, sir, I am drunk, and there is no possible doubt about it," the student replied. "Would you allow me to sit down?"

Without waiting for permission, he plopped into the armchair.

"What do you want from me?" I asked.

"Everything ... and nothing!"

"Perhaps you will prefer to have a good sleep first?"

"Jamais! It is an urgent matter."

"Speak."

"You see, sir, I do not even know how to start my story— that's how odd and unusual my case is."

"Come on, come on, tell me already: I value my time."

The student hiccupped and began to speak in a somewhat thick voice:

"I once read in a newspaper that a young man was needed for two months for performing secretary duties at a good rate. Good. Great, even! I went to the place at the indicated address. I was received by a gentleman of a very decent appearance, who talked to me for about ten minutes and hired me, offering a hundred rubles a month. At first, everything was good, but then I started noticing many weird things about his behavior. He would peer at me for long times, like he was studying my appearance. Once, when we went to a bathhouse, he looked at my body especially closely and then rubbed his hands and whispered in a barely audible voice, 'Nice, clean body, no birthmarks or other distinctive things ....' That's right, sir, no birthmark or other distinctive things, i.e., rien, isn't it strange?

In a few days, he and I went to Kiev, staying in one room in a nice hotel.

The entire day we were running around the city with different tasks and things we needed to buy, so when we came back to the hotel in the evening, I wanted to rest.

I got undressed and lay down. My boss sat at the desk to write a letter, and he suddenly tells me:

'Would you try the jacket on? If it fits you, I will gladly present it to you.'

I tried it on, and, imagine that, the jacket fit me perfectly, like it had been made for me. My boss was happy, and he immediately told me I could keep the jacket. Finally, I fell asleep. I do not know for how long I was sleeping, but I suddenly woke up under the heaviness of a gaze. I slightly opened my eyes, and I saw my boss was watching me.

I closed my eyes again, but so that I still was able to watch him. For approximately ten minutes, he stared intently at me. Then, I started to deliberately snore, so he must have thought I was asleep. He quietly got up, came up to the suitcase by his bed, and took a couple of long knives out of it, like this long," he showed the size with his hands. "He did all this quietly, carefully, and without tearing his eyes away from me. I was gripped by wild terror. I opened my eyes, slightly rose from the bed, and put my feet on the floor. When he saw me move, he quickly put the knives back. I grabbed my pants, quickly pulled them on, without even putting long johns on, and having barely buttoned my pea jacket, I ran out under the excuse of an upset stomach. I rushed headlong to the train station (fortunately, I had money with me) and got into a train. So today, upon my arrival in Moscow, I celebrated my escape from an indubitable danger and came to you in order to tell about this utterly strange incident."

"Why did you run away? What were you afraid of?"

"How about the knives?"

"What would be his interest in killing you?"

"How should I know? But the way he looked at me, sir, the way he looked at me, it made me think he wanted me to be him, and him to be me."

"Oh, my friend, I think you've just let your tongue run away with you. What kind of rubbish is it? 'Me to be him, and him to be me? That was simply your dream."

"How could it have been a dream, if I even left my luggage there!"

"What was in your luggage?"

"Well, a silver soap box, for one thing."

"What else?"

"Well, the towel, long johns, and the jacket that was given to me as a present."

I thought for a moment and asked:

"Where do you live in the city?"

"Nowhere, so far, but before I lived there and there." He gave me the addresses and his name.

I made an inquiry on the phone, and what he had said was confirmed.

"What was the address of the place you went for the secretary job interview?"

"I can't remember that, but maybe I will tomorrow, after having a good sleep."

"All right. If you do, come back here. Goodbye!"

The student hesitated for a while, and then muttered:

"Sir, I certainly understand that my information is of little value, but perhaps you will lend me three rubles anyway? And I will remember the address and let you know."

"Please, have it." I held a three-ruble bill out to him.

The student snatched it and showered me with his thanks:

"Thank you so much for this; oh, I will drink a nice one to your health. Vivat to the sir! Gaudeamus igitur," he unconfidently bowed and left the office.

I briefly jotted down the information he provided and hid the paper, just in case, in the special drawer.

He didn't come the next day, so soon I forgot he existed.

After about five days, the chief of Petrograd Police Vladimir Gavrilovich Filippov called me on the phone:

"A rather mysterious murder occurred here on Leshtukov Lane, Arkady Frantsevich. In a furnished accommodation a dead body was found, headless, wearing a new, well-made jacket. The corpse's head was found in the oven, severely mutilated (cheeks are cut out, ears are cut off, forehead is skinned). There was an attempt to burn the head, apparently, but it failed. After examining the jacket we found out that it was made by a Moscow tailor named Jacques. I hope you wouldn't mind sending an agent to him with the information that I will now dictate to you. Just in case, a fabric sample will be brought to you today by a functionary I sent with a fast train. And he will also report the examination details to you."

Then Filippov dictated to me some figures and terms that 'expert' tailors had provided him.

Of course, I promised him full assistance and immediately sent an agent to tailor Jacques. There it was found out that a jacket of such size, quality, and color had been recently made for a certain engineer named Andrei Gilevich, for 95 rubles.

When I heard the name Gilevich, I gave a start, since I well knew this character thanks to a recent cunning fraud with a fake soap company, into which Gilevich managed to draw many people and significant capital. At the Moscow Police, we had both a photograph of this big swindler and a sample of his handwriting. Previously, Gilevich had made a most disgusting impression on me, and I pictured him in my head as a typical Lombroso's 'character.'

I immediately called Filippov and passed him the information I had gotten from Jacques. I also added that I had grounds to suppose that it was not Gilevich who had been killed and that it seemed like a frame-up. Considering that Gilevich had a big birthmark on his right cheek, the fact the face was mutilated strengthened my suspicions.

V.G.Filippov thought the circumstances of the murder were odd, too, so he decided not to bury the body for a while, and energetically set to the investigation.

I questioned the man who had come from Petersburg with the fabric sample, and from his story I learned that in the search of the murdered person's room, two long knives were found and a silver soapbox with a monogram 'A.'

When I heard about the knives and the soapbox, I remembered at once the drunk student. I raked through the drawer, found the note in it with his testimony and address, and rushed to his place. As I found him hopelessly drunk, snoring in a deep sleep, I ordered that he be taken to the police station. He slept on the couch for a few hours. When he awoke, he was given something to eat and to drink, and then he appeared before me.

"You know what? Why don't you describe the soapbox you forgot in Kiev to me?"

"Ah, sir, I feel so bad! Honestly, I kept trying to remember the address of this guy, but I never did."

"All right, we'll talk about it later. What did your soapbox look like?"

"An ordinary one, a box with a lid …."

"Was there any image on the lid?"

"No, just a letter."

"Which letter?"

"A."

"Why 'A'?"

"You see, it wasn't my soapbox, it was my pal's. Although, I was going to return it, but it so happened I never had to."

"Now please be so kind to remember the address of the place you went for the secretary job interview."

"I swear I'd be glad to remember, but, as ill luck would have it, I had a lapse of memory."

"In this case I won't let you out of here. Remember, please."

The student started to think intensely, rubbing his forehead, rolling his eyes, and suddenly his face brightened with a smile.

"Yes, yes, I remember!" he said joyfully. "Third Yamskaya-Tverskaya St., I do not know the number of the building, but I can recognize it and show you."

"Great. Let's go this instant!"

On Third Yamskaya-Tverskaya St. the student at once pointed at some furnished accommodation. It was held by a certain woman named Pesetskaya. She recognized him and even asked him about his former companion. She told me in detail that a certain Pavlov lived in her accommodation, and that a lot of young people were coming to him regarding his job openings. After he finally hired "him over there" (she nodded at the student), he and his secretary moved out after a few days. In about a week Pavlov came back, but alone this time. Different students came to his place, and again he hired one, and left for Petersburg with him about a week ago. "Although I can check the book and give you the exact time of all departures and arrivals."

"Take a look a this photo, is that Mr. Pavlov?" I said, showing her Gilevich's picture, which I had taken from the official archives.

"That's him, him for sure!" Pesetskaya and the student confidently said.

I had no doubt left that the murder in Leshtukov Lane was Gilevich's doing. However, the motive for the murder remained unclear to me. What could make Gilevich do such a horrible thing? It didn't seem like either mercenary or vengeful motives guided him. Then what were the stimuli to drive his criminal will? A sexual perversion, a sadistic inclination? But then why would he need to put his own jacket on the dead body? What was the precise mutilation of the murdered man's face for?

At this moment V.G.Filippov called me again on the phone:

"You know," he said to me, "your assumption concerning Gilevich didn't prove right. I summoned Gilevich's mother and brother to see the corpse, and they both recognized their son and brother Andrei. The mother was crying over her deceased son without a moment of doubt about his identity. I guess we will have to conduct the investigation some other way."

In response to this I told V.G.Filippov what I had found out, and I persuaded him not to trust Gilevich's mother and brother.

The next issue was to establish the identity of the victim.

I wrote to all of the presidents of Moscow's institutions of higher education, asking them to provide me with precise information about the students who had taken long-term academic leaves within the previous two weeks. Along with this request, I provided a description of the murdered student, i.e., his large stature and thick, big-boned build. Soon the offices of the institutions sent me the requested lists, about 30 names overall. I sent agents to all the addresses received, and I myself started to examine their reports.

Out of 30 reports, there were only 2 that drew my attention. One said that Nikolay Alexeyevich Krylov, a student, left for Petrograd on such-and-such date, and the other one said that Alexander Prilutsky, a student, found an occupation and went to Petrograd for two months, having reserved his room in Moscow. I rushed to the place, the address of which was in the latter report.

The landlady gave a good reference for Prilutsky: a humble, meek man, of modest means, but paying punctually. She said that he had found a job and left for two months. He kept the room and had paid for a month in advance. He had locked his stuff in the room and had taken only a small suitcase.

I called for agents and started a thorough search. After studying Prilutsky's correspondence, we found out that he was an orphan and only had one family member, his aunt who lived in a small manor in Smolensk Province.

I immediately sent an agent to the manor, having given him photos of the corpse and the dead head.

Upon his return, the agent reported that Prilutsky's aunt had received a letter from the latter about two weeks earlier from Moscow, and in the letter he gladly informed her that he had been hired as a secretary by a certain Pavlov and that he was leaving for Petrograd with him. The aunt was profoundly struck and saddened by the thought of her nephew's possible death.

She could not positively identify her nephew in the photos of the murdered man shown to her, but she found a lot of resemblance in the structure and arrangement of teeth. The aunt also said that the man's deceased father, as he had worried about his son's education, deposited 5,000 francs under his name with one of Paris's banks, hoping that his son would go to Paris for improvement in the sciences.

With the information received, it was clear that it was Prilutsky who had been murdered.

But the same damned question kept torturing me: Why did Gilevich need to commit this murder? It was not the 5,000 francs that tempted him. He hadn't known Prilutsky before. Obviously, Prilutsky fell victim due to his resemblance with Gilevich only. More and more often the words of the drunk student came to my mind:

"He wanted me to be him, and him to be me!"

When I passed the additional information I had received to Filippov, I learned that he had some interesting new data regarding the case.

He had contacted insurance companies, and he found that Andrei Gilevich's life was insured for 250,000 rubles in a "New York" insurance company. It turned out that Gilevich's mother had already submitted the insurance policy to receive the insurance premium.

So that is what the mysterious transformation of dead Prilutsky into 'murdered Gilevich' was needed for!

Filippov, of course, arrested Gilevich's mother and brother, but the brother hanged himself in prison, and it was only the mother left behind the bars.

What was left now was to find the murderer. However, it proved to be a rather difficult thing to do, for he could have easily hidden abroad.

Most thorough searches resulted in nothing. I was about to lose my patience, when I suddenly received the following letter from Prilutsky's aunt:

"Dear Sir, Mister Chief-

I think it my duty to inform you on the following circumstance, which will possibly assist you in solving the utterly disquieting case of disappearance of my nephew, Alexander Prilutsky. Yesterday I received a letter from Paris, allegedly signed by Sasha[8], in which he asked me to send necessary documents to the Central Post Office of Paris to be called for.

He needs those in order to withdraw the deposit that was submitted under his name by his father. Although the handwriting in the letter does look like Sasha's, I still have doubts about its authenticity.

Besides, I cannot admit the thought that Sasha, who was always good about keeping me informed of his situation and plans, could go to Paris without giving me notice beforehand. Please, sir, figure out this case, as complicated and possibly horrible to me as it is, and may God help you in this!"

According to my order, the expert examination of the letter forwarded to me and Gilevich's autograph kept in our archive was carried out, and their identity was pronounced. Especially alike were the capital A's.

So, Gilevich was in Paris!

After discussing the matter with V.G.Filippov, we decided to send an extremely talented and efficient functionary, M.N.K., to Paris to detain Gilevich. M.N.K. received my instructions and went to Paris.

I was vexed when the day after his departure an article appeared in Novoye Vremya about M.N.K.'s departure to Paris and about the goal of his trip. I immediately sent an urgent telegram after him, informing him about the article and offering to buy up all the Paris such-and-such date issues of Novoye Vremya.

Having received my telegram upon his arrival to Paris, M.N.K. managed to buy up all the newspaper's issues at the Gare du Nord, and there were only two or three that managed to enter the market. Immediately, M.N.K. rushed to the Central Post Office, where he learned that a gentleman had received the called-for

---

[8] Sasha is a diminutive for Alexander.

correspondence from Russia on the previous day. What was left, therefore, was the bank. There, fortunately, the money deposited under the name Prilutsky was not yet withdrawn by anyone. M.N.K. warned the teller and asked him to immediately inform him as soon as anyone came for that money. In two days the teller let him know about such a request, and M.N.K. saw some stranger who didn't look like Gilevich at all. He let him receive the money and arrested the stranger with the assistance of French police when the stranger was coming out of the bank. The arrested man was taken to the police commissariat, where it was found that he was an artfully made up Gilevich. When his glued-on beard and wig were taken off, and when the makeup was washed off his face, there was no doubt left about the arrested man's identity.

There was a point when the murderer attempted to convince French police that Russian authorities were persecuting him as a political offender, but no one, of course, took his words seriously.

As he saw that he had lost the game, Gilevich confessed to everything.

He was taken from the bank to the commissariat with his small suitcase that he, apparently, had with him since he had come straight from the train station.

Now, after acknowledging his guilt, he asked for permission to wash himself thoroughly again in view of his having makeup on recently. He received permission, so he took a towel and a piece of soap from his suitcase and went to the restroom under the escort of a policeman. In the restroom, he adroitly put a chopped-off little piece of soap into his mouth, filled his cupped hands with water, and quickly washed the soap down. Before the policeman could yank him away, Gilevich dropped dead.

It turned out he kept potassium cyanide in his soap, so it was that which he swallowed at the crucial moment.

According to Filippov's order, Gilevich's body was embalmed and sent to Petersburg.

That is how one of the gravest criminals of our time ended his earthly life.

The skillful lawyer who defended Gilevich's mother achieved her acquittal.

But does human justice with its acquittals and punishments matter to a mother, if she, to heaven's nemesis, lost two grownup sons to a noose and poison?

A Freakish Woman

I ordered a poster to be hung in the receiving room of the Moscow Police, saying that the chief of police receives from such-and-such to such-and-such hour, but in cases that allow no delay, he receives at any time of day and night.

Once, in early spring, I stayed at my office until midnight, as I was dealing with a number of urgent cases, when suddenly I heard a car pulling over near the station. In a while, the functionary on duty reported.

"Sir, there is a lady in mourning wishing to see you."

"Me? At this hour?"

"Yes. I offered her the standard procedure to submit an application, but she pointed at the poster and said that the case allowed no delay, so she wished to address you immediately."

I shrugged my shoulders in vexation.

"Well, all right, let her in."

A middle-aged woman, quite good-looking, all in black, with a crepe on her head, entered my office, came up to the table, and fell into the chair. She covered her face with a handkerchief and started crying before she said anything.

"Please, madam, calm down. Do not worry and tell me what the matter is."

The lady kept crying, and soon she got hiccups and began to nervously giggle—in short, all the signs of hysterics. I hurriedly offered her a glass a water, gave her some time to calm down, and then asked again:

"Tell me, what happened?"

"Ah, my sorrow is boundless, I am so stunned."

"I am listening, madam, please speak."

"Sir, my cat Alfred is missing!"

I was so surprised that I opened my mouth wide, and my eyes bulged, and a wave of indignation arose in my heart.

"You crazy fool!" I thought, but I had no time to say anything before my odd visitor started to chatter impetuously, hopelessly, and breathlessly:

"Yes, sir, a marvelous, wonderful, incomparable Siberian cat, with those big green eyes and huge fluffy whiskers," the lady goggled and puffed her cheeks, trying to show all the beauty of the missing cat.

"Listen, madam, do you really think I have time to deal with trifles like this? Submit an application to my office, and measures for searching for your cat will be taken."

"Ah, how can you, sir, call the grief that fell upon me a trifle? How is that a trifle if I cannot eat, or sleep, and have lost my peace completely? Do you know that I loved my Alfred more than I love my husband, more than everything (the lady gave a hysterical squeal)? And how could one not adore him? For not only was he a pretty one, but also amazingly smart. Ah, sir, how smart he was! I would say to him, "Alfred, hop on my shoulder," and he immediately gracefully bent his back, waved his tail, jumped like a tiger, and was on my shoulder in the twinkling of an eye!"

"Listen, madam," I started, but she interrupted me.

"I did take good care of him, sir, of my sweet little cat! Not only did I carefully look after his stomach, but also tried to divine all his desires."

The lady started crying again.

"Then, maybe, no one has stolen him?" I said, repressing a smile. "But he just left you and now is wandering somewhere on the roofs. Don't forget, madam, it's March!"

My visitor looked at me scornfully, shrugged her shoulders, and said dryly, but with dignity:

"My Alfred would never do anything that mean to me."

I pressed a button and called agent Nikiforov to the office.

There was a so-called flying squad of around 40 people at the Moscow Police. It consisted of specialists in different spheres of investigation. Namely: horse guys, cow guys, dog guys and cat guys, shops guys and theater guys—depending on their field. A reader might find the existence of such a unit strange, but it's necessary because, first of all, larcenies dramatically differ by the ways they are committed, and, second, the places where stolen things are dealt in differ, too. Therefore, it is quite important to have agents who are specialists in their own fields.

Nikiforov, whom I called, was a cats and dogs guy, and he displayed remarkable talents in what he did. It was like nature itself created him for this role. There was even something canine about his appearance: very bent legs, like those of a dachshund, a habit of tilting his head when he listened, and the tendency to noticeably move his ears when he was excited.

I described the missing cat and ordered Nikiforov to work especially hard this time.

After a lot of tears, invocations and imploring, the lady finally left my soul to rest. When I arrived at home, I was exhausted and sank into a deep sleep.

I saw Alfred in my dreams.

The next morning, right after I arrived at my office, I was greeted by Nikiforov, who entered with a big bundle.

Alfred was found!

When I untied the bundle on my desk, I saw a truly charming Siberian cat, who bent his back into a wheel, and started yawning with his small pink mouth and silently mewing.

"Where should I put him?" Nikiforov asked.

"Well, put him in an empty cell for now, but don't forget to close the window."

"Yes, sir."

I called the lady on the phone and asked her to come and take found Alfred. All I heard in the receiver was a cordial cry.

In a quarter on an hour she came rushing by car and stormed into my office, all shining.

"Oh, thank you, thank you, sir! I knew I had to ask you! I knew there was nothing impossible for you. Is it for real, is my Alfred found?!" she strongly shook my hand. "But where is he?"

"He will be brought now. He has been in a cell."

"Oh! A cell! Sir!" she said reproachfully and slowly.

"I couldn't have kept him in my bosom, madam, could I?!"

"Of course not, but still!"

It's hard to describe her wild joy at the moment when Nikiforov came in, lovingly holding Alfred in his arms. There were terms of endearment, mad kisses, squeezing, and pressing to the heart. Alfred displayed his outstanding intelligence at once and clearly recognized his mistress.

"Sir, please let me thank your dear, sweet, nice Nikiforov."

"Please, madam, I do not mind—"

How surprised was I when she took out a five hundred-rubles bill, asking to pass it to Nikiforov.

"No, no, madam, I cannot accept such an amount: You will spoil my people. Besides, do you want your Alfred to disappear tomorrow again? No, do not lead anyone into temptation."

Finally we agreed on 100 rubles, and Nikiforov, gladdened with such an unexpected reward, moved his ears a lot that day.

A Few Dear Portraits

Being the chief of the Moscow Police has a very special feature: By its nature, not only does this attract people of different social statuses, but it also attracts people for quite diverse and often curious reasons. The Chief of Detectives frequently finds himself to be a sort of confessor and confidant of human souls, but even more frequently he has to listen to series of ridiculous complaints. How many types of visitors pass before him! I have already described a freakish woman with a cat in one of the previous stories. But here are some more curious portraits of my occasional visitors.

A scatterbrain

"Sir, there is a man wishing to see you."

"What does he want?"

"He wouldn't say."

"Well. Let him in."

A man with the appearance of a merchant walked into my office with measured steps. He searched for an icon with his eyes; when he found one, he slowly crossed himself, made a bow almost from the waist, and hesitatingly approached the table.

I pointed at the armchair.

"Please, sit down!"

"No worries, we can stand."

"Why would you stand? Sitting conversations go smoother. Sit down! Sit down, will you?"

My visitor sat down on the edge of the armchair, stroked his ginger shovel-like beard, and looked at me with meek, touched, bluish eyes. The room was filled with a peculiar and rather complicated smell: a mixture of tar, sweat, tea, and black bread.

"So, what are you going to tell me?"

He cleared his throat and started his story in a high tenor:

"We come from Yaroslavl. Working in the trading.

"We make no huge gains, but, just so you know, I'd be a sinner if I said we didn't have enough. And today, too, by the way, I brought a carful of veal to Mother Moscow, and managed to sell it with no loss. This is good!

"So I decided to treat myself to some tea. What can I say, that was what I wanted! I went to this tavern, it's called Anchor. And I should say we'd heard some stories of those taverns of Moscow: Not only will you be robbed blind, but also stolen yourself and sold to gypsies unless you really watch out. So, all right! I enter and think to myself, 'Look alive, Mitrich, look alive, 'cause you never know!'

"So this servant in the cloakroom goes like:

'You better take your fur coat off, merchant, 'cause you'll sweat through it!'

"That rogue,' I am thinking. 'He thinks I am a stupid fool! Like I'm buying it!'

'That's all right, my friend, we're used to it,' I said.

"And that fur coat of mine was dignified, with a broad beaver collar—I say, topnotch. 'Cause there's no way the likes of us can show up in Moscow without something like this. The business requires it. And for the sake of deserving credit, too, you know. So, I was saying, I enter this place and sit at a table, but I don't take the coat off. Then I had a potful and one more, and really sweated.

"So I thought I could throw the coat on the back of the chair, and sit on it, just to be sure —I mean, what could possibly happen to it in that case? It will just stay with me, surely. So I did that.

"And I got to such kindly and balanced state, your most honorable sir, I cannot even describe it. I felt free without the coat, and I had sold the calves well, so I felt light and joyful at heart. I had another couple of potfuls, without any haste, paid the servant, and even gave that swindler ten kopecks extra, so I got up to put the coat on and then: what? Mother of God! The collar was gone! I started dashing back and forth and asking waiters, but they only laughed:

'You should've left it at the doorkeeper's, merchant, and that'd be safe!'

"I bet it was those swindlers themselves who cut it. Those packs of cheats of Moscow! As long as I live I won't forget it, and I'll command my grandchildren to remember it! For God's sake, sir, have the collar found! 'Cause I paid two hundred rubles for it, may I drop dead!"

Brazen

It became known to the police that after serving a term of banishment, a certain artful cardsharp named Prutyansky had returned to Moscow. According to the obtained data, Prutyansky was back to his old ways, so I ordered a search of his hotel room. The search resulted in nothing.

So I naturally forgot about this trifle.

The next morning I was informed that some official in a uniform wanted to see me.

"Let him in."

The door of my office opened noisily, and a tall, stately gentleman with his head proudly raised, wearing a uniform coat of the Chancellery of Empress Mary and with a uniform cap in his hands, quickly came up to my desk, carelessly threw the cap onto it, and plopped into the armchair without waiting for an invitation.

"How can I help you?"

"For God's sake, sir! Devil knows what is going on! Yesterday your people stormed into my place at a hotel, turned it into a mess, and left without even apologizing. How can that be? It is impossible that anyone can break into your dwelling like this with impunity! I might complain about you to the authorities in Petersburg, unless you manage to control your idiots!"

"What is your name?"

"Prutyansky, collegiate councilor," he replied nonchalantly.

I had already been extremely enraged by the visitor's brazen tone, and when I heard his name, the name of a well-known police-registered cardsharp, I lost control, banged my fist on the desk with all my strength, and yelled:

"Out! Get out right now, you brazen trash! I'll throw your brazen butt out of my office, and I'll throw it out of Moscow too in no time! Out, I said!"

I got up and moved toward him. Brazen people are usually as cowardly as they are brazen. It was fully proved with Prutyansky. Forgetting his cap on the desk, he dashed toward the exit, looking back at me in fright, and started to scratch on the door of a closet next to the exit, trying to open it.

"Hey, stop trying to get into my closet! You're harming state property!" I yelled, stomping.

Finally, the collegiate councilor got out of the office, leaving traces of his extreme agitation on the parquet.

A reveler

One night, I was suddenly awakened by a telephone.

"Hello, I am listening," I said hoarsely.

A half-drunken voice sounded in the receiver:

"Put me through to the main chief of all the police of Moscow and … its districts!"

"This is he, speaking. How can I help you?"

"This is Semechkin, collegiate registrar, speaking."

"Nice to meet you."

"Me, too-o-o!"

"What do you want from me?"

"What do you mean what do I want? For God's sake, sir! God knows what's going on here! I say to this later … this wa-a-aitor, 'Gimme another carafe of vodka,' and he goes like, 'It's already late, they no longer serve it at the counter.' So, what does this 'late' mean anyway, when, strictly speaking, it's actually early …. Then again, Lily is here. So that guy like comper … comer … compromises me in her eyes. I mean, that's not right … What do you think?"

"Sure, sure! You're absolutely right. Where exactly are you being compromised like this?"

"What? Don't you know that? 'Cause you're like the main chief of all districts! That's odd!!"

"Of course I knew, but I have forgotten."

"At the Elephant, the Elephant, shame on you!"

"And where are you, in the main room or in a private room?"

"What kind of question is that?! The main room, of course! My Lily wouldn't ever gad about private rooms. To the right from the exit: me, Lily, and my pal, Ladonov ... But he really shouldn't count on .... No, he won't have his way with Lily ...."

"All right, wait just a little bit, I will command the owner to give you one more carafe."

"Okay. I will never forget such a favor! Merci!"

Following my order, one of the agents immediately went to the Elephant restaurant, arrested Semechkin, and put him in a police cell for the rest of the night. The next morning we met.

Semechkin turned out to be a consistorian who had just received his first rank and had celebrated the previous night at the Elephant. He was the most good-natured and most harmless man, of about 25, modest and shy.

"For God's sake, sir, please do not make the silly thing I did public! Otherwise I will lose my job, and my wife will kill me!"

"Tell me, mister collegiate registrar, how did you have the guts to bother me in such an impudent way and, moreover, in the middle of the night?"

"God is my witness, I was drunk, drunk as a cobbler! Would I have dared to do so if I had been sober?!"

After reproving him a little bit more, I let Semechkin go, and, of course, I didn't bring a criminal charge against him.

Semechkin's joy was boundless.

An unworthy priest

In 1907, Senator X appealed to the Petrograd police for help. The chief V.G.Filippov was absent, and I, as the assistant, was substituting for him, so I received the senator.

An old man of around 60, looking quite respectable and refined, entered my office, sat in the armchair I offered, looked around cautiously, and spoke in a quiet voice:

"I am addressing you regarding a very ticklish and, of course, confidential matter. A misery has fallen upon my family, and, if you cannot eradicate it completely, you might at least alleviate its grievous consequences."

"At your service, Your Excellency."

The senator gave me an anxious look, and then continued.

"You see, my daughter has escaped." He paused. And then: "But that is only half the trouble. Things happen: youth, romances, love, and all kinds of rubbish like this. But the misery is that her choice is damn strange. If it was some cornet, or hussar, or lawyer, or I could even make my peace with a long-haired student, if worst comes to worst, but it is, if you can imagine, a coachman! A muzhik smelling sour and tarry, and he's dirty, untidy, and lousy!

What's happened to her—I cannot even imagine. Anyway, neither her education nor her environment could have developed such a taste in her. I am at a loss about what the whole thing could be caused by: Is it an erotic madness or the Tolstoy-inspired aspiration to 'become simpler'? Maybe I am out of my mind or hopelessly old-fashioned, turning into a dotard, but I positively refuse to understand the behavior of my dear Nata.

This horse Romeo has whirled her away somewhere, and for several days now I haven't heard a thing from her. I am begging you: Help me find my girl. But please, for God's sake, no publicity, no scandal, for it is important both for her honor and my reputation."

I tried to set the old man's mind at rest as much as I could, promising to start with the searches immediately.

Finding Timothy Tsyganov was not a hard thing to do, since his name was provided to me by the senator, and his street address by the information bureau. I decided to call him to the police station and just talk to him, first.

A sturdy, red-cheeked fellow entered my office. He had a long, black, shovel-like beard, and his hair was abundantly smeared with lamp-oil and cut even all around the head.

"Good day, Timothy!"

"Good day, sir!"

"Listen, pal, what were you thinking?"

"What's this about, sir?"

"Enough with the fooling, Timothy! You know that I'm talking about the senator's daughter."

"Ah, so that's what it is!"

"What else could it be?"

"So what? It's the matter of my happiness, so I guess it just happened!"

"Put happiness aside! Think about it: What are you going to do with her? Is she a match for you?"

"Well, I'll do with her the thing that's always done. And whether she's a match for me or not is really my business."

"Do you think the senator will agree to this?"

"Oh, let him disagree! We don't care!"

"How's that you don't care? He says one word, and you two will be parted."

"Well, that isn't gonna happen! How can a husband and wife be parted against their will? There's not a law for that."

"Are you two married?"

"Of course we are! Entered into a legal marriage."

"Who married you?"

"Simple—a priest did, who else would do it?"

"Of which parish?"

"Well, I just can't seem to remember that," Timothy said sarcastically.

"Stop talking rubbish! In what church did you marry?"

"We don't want to say, and that's it. You find out yourself, if you want."

There was nothing I could do about him, so I let him go and ordered agents to check marriage entries in church registers in all the churches.

It took three days.

By the end of this time, the senator X stopped by my office again. He wanted to know how the investigation went. I told him about my conversation with Timothy. When the old man heard about his newly acquired *beau fils*, he grasped his head and fell into the armchair. After catching his breath and thinking about the situation a little bit, he said sadly:

"Well, if it went as far as the wedding, I guess there's nothing I can do. The only thing left to do is to lick this moron into shape and fix him up with a job somewhere in the backwoods. I don't think I have another choice. Please, sir, forget about the whole sad story and stop the proceedings."

Meanwhile, it became known to us after revising church books that Timothy Tsyganov and the young X were married on such-

and-such date by the father superior of the church of the Lithuanian Prison Castle Vladimir Vozdvizhensky, and the entry in the book was crossed out and there was a marginal note made by Father Vladimir: "Registered by mistake."

One would think that Father Vladimir had smelled out about the alarm concerning this story within past days and had learnt that the young lady he had married was a senator's daughter, so he chickened out and crossed the entry out. At the interrogation, he claimed that he had planned to perform the ceremony and even had prepared the entry in the book beforehand, but he refused to marry them due to the lack of necessary documents and crossed the entry out.

Detailed inquiries I made about Father Vladimir turned out to be horrifying. He apparently was one of those Orthodox priests who didn't believe in God or in the devil and only sought for revenues in their priesthood, trying to gain as much profit as they could by all means. Besides, the private life of Father Vladimir was vicious, too: revels all the time, sometimes even orgies, cards, and women—that was his normal pastime. Among his drinking companions was the sexton of the Lithuanian Castle church, his fellow, a certain Afonov.

The information we had obtained about Father Vladimir surely strengthened our suspicions, so the investigation continued.

The entry in the church register was different handwriting than that of the note made by Father Vladimir in the margin. We found an example of the sexton Afonov's handwriting, and the authorship of the entry was established. Afonov turned out to be an unbelievable coward. We scared him, saying that in case of denial he would be subjected to severe punishment, so he quickly confessed to all and told us everything. Apparently the marriage ceremony was performed for three thousand rubles, and the only document that the bride could show was a business card with a note of recommendation. The participants of the ceremony were Afonov himself and the prison watchman Ivanov. We arrested them both and invited Father Vladimir to the police.

The accused priest, a well-fed man with ginger beard and wavy hair, wearing a silk cassock, was invited to come to the office of V.G.Filippov, as the latter had returned, and I was present, too. The priest was trying to behave amicably, independently, and piously.

"Congratulations on the good weather!" he said, stretching out his hand and waving it vaguely.

"Please sit down, Father."

"Thank you, with great pleasure!"

"So, Father, is it true that you never married them and the marriage never happened?"

"My God! How could I have done it with no documents? No, gentlemen, marriage is no joke. Not only do two lives spiritually unify in this sacrament that has been sanctified by the Apostolic Church, but also the obligation is granted to them to intimate approximation of the sexes aimed at prolonging the mankind—"

V.G.Filippov interrupted him:

"Do you know, Father, that at Calvary next to the Savior was a thief hanging on a cross, and here there is a cross hanging on a thief!" he pointed at the father's pectoral cross.

"Interesting," the priest said in a surprised voice, but then pulled himself together, went back to the unctuous tone, and went on. "You of course can insult me here, for I am helpless, but I think it my duty to bring your words to the Right Reverend's notice."

"So, Father, are you positive you didn't marry them?"

"May I lose my priesthood if I am lying!" Father Vladimir got up, turned to the icon, and crossed himself with a wide gesture.

"Semyonov!" I shouted. "Bring Afonov in."

The door opened, and the confused figure of the sexton appeared on the threshold.

He grinned in an idiotic way and suddenly announced in a joyful voice to Father Vladimir.

"You know, Volodya[9], I have confessed!"

---

[9] Volodya is a diminutive for Vladimir.

"Bastard, that's who you are," the Father said dryly, but convincingly.

For his marriage speculation, Father Vladimir was defrocked and sentenced to one and a half years of penal labor.

The Seminarian Gang

Some tough months fell to my lot in 1913.

Moscow was being terrorized by a series of armed robberies accompanied by murders. The robberies followed one after another with intervals of a week or two and definitely bore common signs: Victims were cleaned out (frequently left in their underwear) and always murdered by a bladed weapon. Out of the cycle of murders, the following, near the end of the case, are especially engraved in my memory.

The murder of a flirting couple going to Sparrow Hills to the Krynkin's restaurant: Not only were the passengers robbed and killed, but also the cabman who had taken them. The murder of the rich merchant Belostotsky behind the Dragomilovskaya Zastava Square and severe wounding of his relative in the same cab. Finally, an atrocious murder of two old women in the village of Bogorodskoye near Moscow.

This last murder was especially horrible. The victims lived in Bogorodskoye in a small, old rectory. One of them was the widow of a local priest. Her elderly sister lived with her. Not only were both women killed, but also subjected to precise torture before death. The appearance of their corpses chilled the blood: broken bones, breasts cut out, and charred heels testified of the monstrous torture they had been through.

The house was a wreck. Everything that could be taken out had been taken out. In short, it was the same picture of cleaning out that had become so familiar after the series of recent cases.

Near the house were the dead bodies of two poisoned dogs.

I listed only three cases, but within three of four months, there had been over ten crimes that were committed, obviously by the same gang.

After the first two similar unsolved cases, I got all of the detective police actively involved. They did everything they could. Thieves and frauds registered on our lists were interrogated. All the common locations of dealing in stolen goods were searched. Dozens of agents spent days and nights in all kinds of bars and dens that were often visited by the criminal world of Moscow; the hope was to catch at some thread at least to put us on the trail.

However, none of our actions were successful.

Just as bad was the situation with roundups and ambushes.

In the end, I came to the conclusion that it was the doing of a gang of nonprofessionals—of people who had never been handled by the detective police and were distant from the ordinary criminal elements of Moscow. Such deduction didn't help me move forward much, and with every new display of activity of the brazen gang I became very nervous, as I realized the necessity to reveal and destroy the newly born criminal organization at any cost.

But what was I to do? My people were run off their legs. I myself was exhausted after painful searching for the key to this puzzling riddle.

And there came, slowly prowling, the doubt of my strength creeping into my soul. The faith in myself started fading away.

But I drove this momentary weakness away and continued to work hard.

Finally, one and a half months after the holdup behind the Dragomilovskaya Zastava Square, one of the merchants, the one who was severely wounded by the robbers, recovered to such point that I could get a doctor's permission to visit him and ask him questions.

He really survived by a miracle. The wound given to him in the neck near the collarbone turned out quite deep, and it was good fortune that the carotid was not affected.

"Please tell me about the attack which you fell victim to in as detailed way as possible," I said to the wounded man.

"I will, readily, but I do not think I will be of use to you, for there wasn't much I saw or know."

"Please tell me everything you remember."

"I was with my late relative in his cabriolet, just the two of us.

He had just received some money from the bank for paying his workers, as well as some interest-bearing securities. We drove past the Dragomilovskaya Zastava Square, and then the deserted wasteland started. We were silent, each deep in thought, when suddenly five people sprang out from some ditch. Two grabbed the horse's bridle, and one, the leader apparently, shouted to us, "Hey, get out! Now!" My relative got out. I was about to get out too. But then I saw the gang leader jump really close to my relative and knock him down right there by a blow of a knife. Before I could give a cry, another robber, a puny and short one, ran up to me from the right and swung his knife at me. But I managed to draw my revolver, and I shot him point-blank. Frightened and caught off guard, he gave a loud cry, "Oh, devils!" and then howled with pain and grasped his right wrist with his left hand. I suppose I injured his fingers. As the leader saw it, he shouted to him, "Damn you, beer! You can't even stab right!"

"Is it 'beer' you're saying?"

"Yes, beer. Obviously, the thief's nickname. Then another brigand, standing to my left, struck me on the neck with a knife. I fell down, although I didn't pass out. But, as I realized that further resistance was pointless, I pretended to be dead. The brigands robbed and undressed us, and then disappeared. In about an hour I was picked up by random passersby."

The information I received, although it was rather scant, changed my initial assumptions.

'Beer' indubitably was a nickname, and if it was a nickname, then it meant that those we dealt with, even if it wasn't a group of professional murderers, were people close to the common criminal environment.

Having arrived at this conclusion, I immediately sent inquiries to the Petersburg police and all the provincial detective departments, but I received the same answer from everywhere: "No criminal registered under the nickname Beer."

Meanwhile the gang was still in action and unpunished. Another daring murder occurred. A rich ragman was killed and robbed. To be more precise, he was the director and the owner of a whole organization of ragmen.

In this incident one of his workers was wounded too, and he testified that there were four brigands. The picture and the strategy of the robbery were the same. But why then were there four people in action, not five as before? A thought inevitably came to mind that the brigand missing from the gang had to leave it as a result of the hand injury inflicted by Belostotsky's relative defending himself.

I decided to publish in all newspapers a letter addressed to doctors, asking them to inform the chief of Moscow Detective Police if a character of proletarian appearance and puny constitution had seen them within the previous two months for medical assistance concerning his wounded right wrist. Many papers, along with this appeal, described the crimes that the wanted criminal was accused of. At the same time I interrogated doctors in all the county and private hospitals, as well as dispensaries of Moscow Province.

But all in vain.

The Moscow doctors never responded, and the hospitals' response was negative.

I gave myself to despair, which resulted in irritation and blaming the staff for doing nothing. I tried to use their self-esteem, and finally promised a cash bonus to the one who discovered even a single lead in this truly bewitched case.

The case was really unbelievable: After several months of persistent, intense work by the police, there was no result at all.

The stolen things never appeared at flea markets or other marketplaces. The most amazing thing: There wasn't a word from banks, bureaus, and money-changing places that had received detailed lists of stolen interest-bearing securities and coupons. And still the robbers, and they were still in Moscow and still in action, had to get rid somehow of what they had stolen, didn't they?

Of course, it was no secret to me that the White-Stone had fraudulent money-changing places that bought valuables known to have been stolen. But it seemed incredible that somehow not a single coupon made it to circulation or was used for paying third persons at one of Moscow's credit institutions, the more so because the robbers' gang managed to gain a significant amount of interest-bearing securities within that period of time. Securities were stolen from the old women in Bogorodskoye as well as from murdered Belostotsky. Belostotsky's wife testified that on the day of the murder, her husband was supposed to withdraw 50 thousand rubles of a government annuity from his bank deposit to use this money as cover funds for some business. This information was confirmed in the bank, and the exact amount of bank notes, as well as their serial number, was defined. Meanwhile Moscow shut up like a clam and kept silent, dead silent. In my despair, it seemed to me that it was not only Moscow, but the entire country, the entire world, and all the earthly and heavenly powers were against me.

Meanwhile, life went on, bringing to the surface all the froth and scum that are so inherent in big cities with ill-sorted population of many millions. Petty thieves, daring predators, pathetic cheats and brazen swindlers kept marching past me. In this sorrowful succession a certain "doctor" Fedotov flickered across my work.

This "doctor" turned out to be a former military paramedic, an impostor who had appropriated the tile of a doctor of medicine and practiced illegal abortions. At the arrest, he pled guilty and desired to see me for some reason. I called him over to my office.

"What do you have to say, Fedotov?"

"I sort of wanted, mister chief, to ask you for something: Would you please be so kind to ease my tough lot from here on out? If so, I will give you some information."

"All right, Fedotov, I will order my agent to highlight your full and frank confession. This is the most I can do."

"Please do so!"

"I will do what I can. What was that you wanted to inform me about?"

"You see, a while before my arrest I read your appeal to doctors in a newspaper."

"So?"

"Well ... about two months ago, a man came to me who looked like the one you described. His fingers were wounded and so neglected that gangrene had started. It was impossible to save them, so I amputated them, all five of them."

"Where does he live?"

"I don't know that."

"What's his name?"

"He said his name was Frenchman. He also said he had wounded his hand at a brewery, where he allegedly worked."

"Brewery, you say?"

"Right, brewery."

I immediately remembered the phrase, "Damn you, beer! You can't even stab right!"

And behind the Dragomilovskaya Zastava Square, quite close to the spot of Belostotsky's murder, there was a big brewery. Obviously, it was possible now to get the process moving and put the investigation on the right trail.

"Then why didn't you report when you read the appeal?" I asked Fedotov.

He bashfully smiled and said:

"Because you, mister chief, appealed to doctors. How am I really a doctor?"

"Can you give me any more information regarding this?"

"I think I said all I knew. Unless ... he gave me a coupon as payment for my work."

"Right now, go home with two inspectors and bring this coupon."

We checked it and found out that the coupon was from the thousand-rubles annuity that belonged to the priest's widow from Bogorodskoye. This fact proved once again that those were the same criminals that took part in the robberies of Belostotsky and the old women in Bogorodskoye, so I was on the right track.

According to the Moscow information bureau, there were around 20 people named Frenchman, but they all turned out to be respected men who disarmed any suspicion. Nor was the information I received from the provinces successful.

I went to the brewery behind the Dragomilovskaya Zastava Square and asked the staff manager about a worker named Frenchman. The manager burrowed into his lists and told me that they didn't have a worker named Frenchman and had never had one. A nimble office boy that was hanging around heard our conversation and suddenly blurted:

"This Kolya[10] French guy worked here at wash."

"Is that his name?" I asked.

"No," the boy replied. "His name was Fortunatov, and French was just a nickname."

"Why did he get this nickname?"

"Simply because he had the French disease."

I asked the manager about Nikolai Fortunatov and learnt that the latter left the job about three month ago and had never showed up at the brewery since then. Interrogated workers told me that he had gone to his home village.

In the same manager's office I leaned that Fortunatov was from a village in the Moscow district.

---

[10] Kolya is a diminutive for Nikolai.

That same day I went there with two agents. We didn't find Fortunatov there.

His parents hadn't seen him for a long time, and they said they didn't even know his address.

However, we conducted a search at their place and found an elegant silk dress trimmed with expensive lace.

Answering my questions where it came from, the old woman told me an implausible story about some lady from Moscow who allegedly gave it to her as a present for many years of honest service of delivering milk, cream, sour cream, and other dairy products. The old woman's story was contradictory and confused, so she finally confessed that it was her son Kolya who gave her the dress. I found it necessary to arrest Fortunatov's parents and detain them at the detective police upon our return to Moscow.

I quickly checked the dress, and it turned out that it belonged to the lady who was killed with her companion and a cabman on their way to Sparrow Hills.

Kolya's parents turned out to be rather sly and cautious peasants.

For two weeks I tried to get Fortunatov's address from them, but they stubbornly pled ignorance.

At last, I decided to resort to "planting."

I ordered Kolya's parents transferred to the police house at Sretensky station, as I pretended that I had given up my attempts to get any information from them and intended to let the judge sort their case now. About three days before their transfer, I sent a female agent in the guise of a thief to the Sretensky police house. The only person who knew about the agent was the house supervisor, who received strict instructions from me not to ease up in any way on my employee.

In a couple of days, for more plausibility, I also transferred there a woman who was a real thief imprisoned at the police station.

After keeping this entire company together for about a week, I released the agent and called for her.

"So?" I asked her.

"The old woman is a real stone. I tried this and that, and she was only silent all the time. But I had a whole week to gain her trust, and I think I did, because, although she told me nothing, when I was leaving she drew me aside and gave me the address of a certain Tanya, Kolya's lover. The old lady is asking Tanya to visit her son and, if he would be so kind, send his folks some tea and sugar to the prison."

My agent went to Tanya and did exactly what the old lady had asked her to do. At the same time, surveillance was set up at Tanya's apartment.

One of my agents, a handsome man disguised as a mailman, came up to Tanya in the street, introduced himself, had a little talk, and soon walked her to Fortunatov's apartment.

That same evening we came there for a search. The criminal behaved very daringly at first.

"Are you Fortunatov?"

"What if I am?"

"You're the one we're looking for."

"What would you need me for?"

"Where do you work?"

"Nowhere. Can you work with a hand like this? I'll even sue those bloodsuckers and oppressors of the poor!"

"All right, French, get dressed!"

"So you know that too already!"

The search at Kolya's place resulted in positively nothing. As I had delivered him to the detective department, I immediately ordered an officer to bring "doctor" Fedotov. The paramedic simply nodded: That was him.

"So, you gave me up, huh?" Kolya asked the paramedic with an evil smile.

"I swear I didn't! I really didn't, no! I am locked up here myself, they grabbed me too."

"Is that true? Locked up? Or maybe you work here? How much do you make?"

"You'll see yourself when we're in the same cell."

"Yeah, right, tell someone else about it! The same cell! I know the trick, so you better not mess with me!"

I interrupted the dialogue.

"Calm down, you won't be doing time together."

The paramedic was taken out.

"Well, Fortunatov, cut the clowning. Confess! Because I know everything."

"What's that you know if there's nothing to know?!"

"Nothing?"

"Nothing!"

"How about the coupon from the murdered old woman in Bogorodskoye?"

"What coupon? What old lady you're talking about?"

"The securities coupon you gave the doctor to amputate your fingers."

"I got this one from some shop as change."

"Which shop?"

"I don't remember."

"Damn you, beer, you can't even stab right!"

After this exclamation, Kolya went pale, sighed heavily, and beads of sweat appeared on his forehead. But he pulled himself together and continued to deny everything. The next day I called for Belostotsky's relative, who had almost completely recovered from the wound, and asked him to take a look at Kolya. However, I warned him that in case he wouldn't recognize the criminal or would be unsure, he shouldn't show that to Kolya.

"You will look at him silently and go to the other room. And you will tell me about the result later."

We did that exactly. Fortunatov was called to my office. The victim, who was already there, looked at him, said goodbye to me, and left the room. I wrote something on a paper, paused a bit, and then followed him, leaving Kolya with two inspectors. Kolya thought that his victim had been dead for a long time, so he of course didn't pay much attention to him.

"So?" I asked the victim.

He made a helpless gesture.

"His stature and shape look similar, but God knows if it's him!"

"Please try to remember."

"How can I remember? If only I could hear his startled cry, because it is still ringing in my ears."

The task was difficult. But I decided to take a shot. I called for an inspector and said:

"When I interrogate him and you are standing behind his back, carefully come up to him and poke his side with two fingers, on a ticklish spot."

The result exceeded expectations.

Kolya, as he was completely engrossed in the interrogation, tensely watching every my word, didn't notice the inspector coming up to him. When he got the poke, he gave a wild cry of surprise and fright, "Oh, devils!"

When he heard it, the victim dashed into the room like a bomb, saying, "Him! Him! No doubt. Same voice, same words, same intonations! That bastard! That scum! Damned murderer!" he attacked Kolya with raised fists. He was dragged to the side. I didn't want to lose the psychologically favorable moment, so I decided to use Kolya's daze: I banged my fist on my desk and shouted to him:

"Come on, confess now! You see, the dead are rising from their coffins to prove you guilty!"

Kolya started tossing about, gave his victim a horrified look, recognized him apparently, his jaw started shaking, and he deliriously spoke:

"Why me? I did nothing. That's him who wounded me—"

"Ah, 'him who wounded me'? Enough."

Kolya realized that he made a slip. He fell on his knees and confessed to everything.

It turned out that the gang that had been terrorizing Moscow for so long consisted of five people. The leader was Sasha Samyshkin, nicknamed Seminarian, and the members were: the brewery's metalworker, a butcher's apprentice, as Kolya called him, Kolya's brother and Kolya himself. Their addresses were given by Kolya, except for the leader's address, as Kolya didn't know it. That day the robbers were arrested, and many things and valuables were found that they had stolen within recent months. They all said horrible things about their leader. According to them, he was not a human being, but a beast: He found pleasure in killing people. Spilling human blood gave him some special sensual delight. According to their testimony, during the murder in Bogorodskoye Sasha the Seminarian tortured his victims for hours. The discipline in the gang was the strictest. Thus, the metalworker once imprecisely executed Sasha's order, and he immediately got a bullet in his chest and was quite severely wounded by it. Apparently, the rest of the criminals hated Sasha, but they feared him even more.

When dividing the plunder, they would gather somewhere in the wasteland, and right on the spot, Sasha would appoint the place, day, and hour of their next meeting. In between the meetings Sasha himself picked the next victim, so when he came to meetings he would only give orders. Disobedience, refusal, or arguing were unthinkable. None of them knew Samyshkin's address.

The arrested murderers were absolute nobodies.

An especially disgusting impression was made by the "butcher's apprentice": medium-sized, with an incredibly broad body, his arms handing virtually down to his knees, he resembled an orangutan.

However, this gorilla gave us a rather valuable direction.

Since a share of interest-bearing securities stolen at the last robbery could not be immediately divided due to their different value, Sasha decided to exchange the securities for money and scheduled settling in five days. And the 'butcher's apprentice' knew that Sasha always carried out his financial operations in the same money-changing shop, at Ilyinka, which he showed us. He supposed that Sasha would inevitably visit it within the next few days as he was going to settle with them.

The criminals described the Seminarian's appearance in detail: tall, handsome swarthy face, small black mustache twisted in a ring, drilling look, shambling. They warned us that Sasha wouldn't surrender alive, and he would inevitably resist by all means.

I immediately set up thorough surveillance on the money-changing shop, making a very experienced inspector Evdokimov, nicknamed 'Khitrov boss', the head of it. To help him, I sent inspector Belkin, remarkable for his immense strength, and ten agents. The agents, disguised as yard keepers, messengers, and cabmen, were on duty for three days. On the fourth day, Sasha showed up.

He was allowed to enter the shop. Evdokimov didn't want to risk people in vain, so he decided to rule out a frontal attack and let Sasha come out of the shop. He let him pass by, but quickly came up to him with Belkin and tightly grasped his left arm, while Belkin grasped the right one. Sasha tried to dash away, but he couldn't.

Then, Sasha resorted to a ruse. He loudly asked passersby for help, pretending to be a victim of some sort of violence or attack. Indeed, the whole thing looked rather strange: a peaceful looking man asking for help and trying to get away from a mailman and a messenger who were hanging onto both his arms and holding him.

I was notified on the phone, and when I came to Ilyinka rushing, I found Evdokimov and Belkin in quite a difficult situation: The crowd clearly sympathized with Sasha and was really pressing the inspectors. I stood up straight in the automobile and loudly shouted:

"I am Chief Koshko of the Moscow police, and I command you to detain this great criminal and murderer immediately!"

The effect was huge: The people flooded back at once. We put Sasha in the automobile and delivered him to Gnezdikovsky Lane. The appearance of Samyshkin had been described quite well. What amazed me about his face was the expression of unshakable will and authoritativeness with a touch of contempt.

"Name?" I asked.

He gave me a drilling look and uttered with pauses:

"I would ask you to speak more politely. Please do not forget I come from intelligentsia just like you do."

"That's a nice intelligentsia you come from, I must say. You're not intelligentsia, but a murderer and the scum of the earth."

Sasha shrugged his shoulders and fell silent. I summoned the "illustrious gathering," i.e., the metalworker, the "butcher's apprentice," and French with his brother, and then I asked for Samyshkin too. The meeting of the leader and his gang was quite curious. Sasha gave them a look full of greatest contempt and evilly whispered:

"So, bastards, gave me up?"

The brigands became indescribably agitated—apparently they feared their leader to death even when his hands were bound. Sasha didn't think it necessary to conceal anything, so he told about all of his crimes in detail and with unbelievable cynicism. It turned out he was the son of a mayor of one of Penza Province's districts' chief towns. Earlier, he had reached the third grade of theological seminary, hence the nickname, apparently. He hated his father and his stepmother, and he openly told me that he had been intending to launch them into eternity in near future. Sasha was incredibly bold.

Soon after the arrest, he attempted to escape. He was being interrogated by my functionary Mikhailov in the latter's office. The office was on the first floor. Due to the heat, the windows were wide open.

A Mauser was before Mikhailov on the desk. When he leaned down to pick something up from the floor, Sasha, his hands bound, quickly sprang toward the desk, grasped the revolver with both hands, stunned Mikhailov by a blow on his head, jumped quickly into the window, and got into the grip of a policeman standing right at the window.

Sasha was sentenced to hang, but because of the amnesty announced in honor of the Romanov dynasty anniversary, his punishment was reduced to 20 years of hard labor.

The February Revolution released Sasha, who said he wanted to go to war. In reality, Sasha came back to Moscow, where he continued to do what he used to do. He didn't forget to get square with the metalworker and the "butcher's apprentice"—he killed both. Sasha somehow displeased the Bolsheviks, and they shot him in 1920 in Moscow.

The Theft in the Dormition Cathedral

This brazen theft happened in the spring of 1910.

In the middle of a sweet sleep, around 4 in the morning, I was awakened by a telephone call.

The functionary on duty provided the information that had just been passed to him by a police officer from the Kremlin. The message was rather alarming: A sentry on duty by the Kremlin Wall near the Dormition Cathedral heard the ringing of breaking glass and noticed a man's silhouette in one of the Cathedral's windows. He shot at it, but without result, apparently. Clerical authorities had already been notified, and they were about to open and search the Cathedral.

Within a minute, I was dressed and rushing to the Kremlin. I reached the Cathedral right before the doors were open. I entered the church along with several police officials. As I set to an initial, superficial search, I at once detected the blasphemous crime: To the left of the royal doors on the solea, close to the iconostasis, was the icon of Our Lady of Vladimir in an enormous case. The case was around eight feet tall and three and a half feet wide, with a door, and it looked more like a cabinet. The icon of Our Lady of Vladimir was Russia's most ancient sacred object and the favorite of the royal family, for with this icon the first of the Romanovs, Tsar Michael I, was blessed for his reign. The icon's gold plating was richly ornamented with precious stones, and especially valuable was the huge square emerald, almost the size of a matchbox, that glowed green among sparkling diamonds.

The examination of the icon showed that the stones, along with pieces of gold plating, were crudely cut out with a sharp instrument and gone without a trace. The icon's painting was not harmed. On the bottom of the case were gold chips and dust, as well as a cigarette butt.

The thief, apparently, had been working inside the case with the door closed to reduce the noise.

I had just finished the search when the powers that be started filling the church. Everyone was there: the mayor, the chief prosecutor, Metropolitan Vladimir, a representative of the palace, and many others. Such extraordinary attention to the incident was not only explained by the theft's scope and brazenness, but also by the interest of the Emperor and the entire royal family.

I decided to start a more thorough search of the Cathedral in order to find out if the criminal himself had hidden in the church or if he had hidden the stolen things in it. Since the Dormition Cathedral is quite large, I ordered about fifty agents to start the examination, headed by special investigator K.

The search was rather tough and took the entire day. Boris Godunov's throne, the patriarchs' tombs, the dome, the roof, and the most concealed parts of the Cathedral were searched, but, alas, it was in vain.

The search of the iconostasis took an especially long time. Strictly speaking, it was not an iconostasis, but a continuous mass of icons that spread in many rows along the Cathedral's southern and northern walls. The icons were fastened together like solid shields. Between the icons' backs and the church's walls was an empty space, about a foot wide. This space was wider in the lower part because, in front of the lower icons, there was a solid shelf, or rather a wide and high step, about two feet in height and one and a half feet in width. All of this empty space was thoroughly searched, up and down and along the walls, with long poles, but it didn't help.

On the right sill of a narrow window above the icons–therefore quite high above the floor–traces of disturbed centuries-old dust were found, but they were rather vague and didn't indicate much.

The glass in the left window was broken, although it was almost an inch thick. This window, like all the other windows in the Cathedral, was so long and narrow that it rather resembled an arrow slit, so it was unlikely that a person could get outside through it.

However, to be sure, I sent my skinniest and smallest agent, who had the body of a child, to examine it, and it turned out that even his frame was twice as wide as the window.

In the evening, by the end of the search, Metropolitan Vladimir came to the church again and asked the investigator K. if the search was over and if the church could be open for regular service. K. responded affirmatively without asking for my opinion and said that the robber, of course, had gotten out of the church. My opinion was exactly opposite.

It is impossible to get out through the windows, and the church's doors had not parted with their forty-pound locks and bolts from the moment the sentry shot at the silhouette in the window and until our arrival; therefore, the thief must still be in the Cathedral, and an ambush should be laid. I shared these thoughts with His Eminence and insisted on cancelling services for a while. Otherwise, I would relieve myself of responsibility for the outcome of the case. My insistence produced its intended effect, and the Metropolitan agreed, although reluctantly, to comply with it.

Telegrams about the theft were immediately sent to Petersburg, and shortly a reply was received from the Minister for Internal Affairs saying that His Majesty commanded that we apply our entire force to finding the items that had been stolen and the one responsible for the theft.

So, I laid an ambush, placing two inspectors and two officers in the Cathedral.

The night passed–nothing. The next day passed–nothing. Another fruitless night passed, and Metropolitan Vladimir sent a person to tell me that the Cathedral needed to reopen. I resisted, and he yielded. Another 24 hours passed with no results, and His Eminence renewed his insistence. With much difficulty, I managed to persuade His Eminence to give me 24 hours more, but after they were gone, he resolutely demanded an end to the ambush. Somehow, I gained several more hours from His Eminence.

That was a hard time for me. Would I really fail on the case that the Emperor himself was interested in, that had the attention of both capitals?

The searches we conducted in Khitrovka, Sukharevka, and other places that dealt in stolen goods didn't provide any results, either. Interrogating professional registered thieves wasn't any more successful. Unfortunately, two significant incidents occurred within those same days: the murder of nine persons in Ipatievsky Lane and the withdrawal of 300,000 rubles from the Province Treasury with counterfeit documents. All this, of course, made the police spread themselves too thin.

I was gloomy, sitting in my office. My professional self-esteem was damaged, and my agitated imagination was painting the most dismal perspectives for me.

The telephone sluggishly rang, and I reluctantly lifted the receiver.

"Who is it?"

"Is that you, sir?"

"It's me. Of course, it's me, for God's sake!" I replied, irritated.

It was the inspector who was watching the Cathedral from the outside, and he told me he had heard shooting in the Cathedral. I rushed to the Kremlin like a bullet with my assistant V. E. Andreev. At the Cathedral's doors, we met one of the inspectors who had been on duty inside it–Mikhailov, a prompt and intelligent fellow.

"What do you have, Mikhailov?"

"Everything is fine; the thief is caught."

"Why were there shots fired? Did he resist?"

"I don't think he could've, sir. He's barely alive due to starvation."

"Then why did you shoot?"

Mikhailov hesitated for a moment, embarrassed, and then asked:

"Do you want me to tell the story in detail?"

"Tell me."

"You see, sir, we relieved our nightshift fellows, and they went to sleep right away, right there under the Tsar Boris's throne.

So they're sleeping, and Dementiev and I were keeping watch, just the way it was ordered–sitting still, no talking. There was dead silence around us. The saints' faces looked at us calmly, and the blue flame of the eternal light shimmered somewhere in the distance. It was only rarely that the silence would be broken by the cracking of a dry tree or the scratching of a mouse near the candle box.

So, we're sitting silently, with the history of Russia living within these walls rushing through our minds. It's like you're sitting under Godunov's throne and thinking: Was there really a time when Tsar Boris sat right here, in this same spot, right above my head? Or you're imagining those tens of thousands of requiems that had been sung here within past centuries. You're looking at the tsar's and the patriarch's seats, and you think you see now the Terrible Tsar, now Nikon the Patriarch, and you kind of feel spooky. I was sitting there and looking at my fellow once in a while, and he had the same feelings on his face.

There was an hour or two of this tension, when suddenly we heard knocking, and again, and again. We started, woke up our sleeping fellows, and the four of us listened intently. The weird noise was consistent, like someone's scratching something or hitting the wall. We looked around, but didn't see anyone and couldn't understand where the sounds were coming from. And yet, the sounds were growing louder and louder. I crossed myself, and Dementiev started to whisper a prayer. We pressed ourselves together and stared at the iconostasis. Suddenly a terrible thing happened: One icon fell off the very top row and banged against the tiles of the stone floor.

A humming sound started by this crash went all around the cathedral and froze somewhere in the dome. The repetitive noise stopped for a moment, and dead silence fell. Our hearts hammered, our throats squeezed, and our mouths dried up. Suddenly, something appeared in the spot where the icon had fallen. We couldn't make out what it was, but it was something horrible, like a gray lump in the shape of a man, but without eyes, nose, mouth, or ears. We gave a wild cry and started shooting with our Mausers, randomly, without aiming, at the scary ghost. After the first shot, it slipped down, trying to catch at the icons, and stretched out on the floor. It was only then that we realized it was a human being before us.

Our bullets didn't get him, but there was another terrible accident: One of the bullets punched a hole in the Saint Pantaleon icon. We caught the fallen man, and then you came."

I entered the church and went straight to the thief. His appearance amazed me. Indeed, he rather looked like a ghost, not like a living man. His head, face, arms, and clothes were covered with a thick, fluffy layer of centuries-old dust. The "one in grey" could hardly stand and looked pathetic.

The news about catching the sacrilegious thief spread around Moscow quickly, and crowds of people, burning with a thirst for revenge, poured toward the Cathedral, wishing to take over justice and finish the impudent defiler of sacredness themselves. My people reported this to me, claiming that taking the thief out of the Cathedral through the main door, past the droning crowd, was unthinkable. He would inevitably be torn apart by the indignant people. After hesitating for a while, I decided to take the thief out through the back door with V. E. Andreev, through the Tainitskiye Gate, and then take a horse-driven cab instead of a car, while K. was waiting for us at the Kremlin Square. The trick worked, and we successfully brought the criminal to Malyi Gnezdikovsky Lane.

There, I immediately ordered that some of my eldest son's clothes be brought. The thief was allowed to wash and change. He said his name was Sergei Semin, and he was a jeweler's apprentice.

"So, Seryozha[11], you hungry?"

He didn't answer, but the thought about food made him shake, and he started to swallow his saliva.

From the nearest restaurant, two portions of shchi, two cutlets, and a huge loaf were delivered.

For the first time in my life I witnessed a truly starving man eating. He swallowed the shchi greedily, stuffing his mouth with

---

[11] Seryozha is a diminutive for Sergei

unbelievable pieces of meat, tearing the bread, and in about five minutes, he completely destroyed all the food.

"You want more?"

"I do, if you be so kind!"

"Won't it kill you after all the starving?"

"That's okay. I'll finish it, just fine!"

He was given one more cutlet and more bread.

"So, Seryozha, shall we have some tea now?"

"With great pleasure, mister chief!"

We were given tea, and I had a cup with him.

Meanwhile some Moscow authorities came to our office to take a look at this rare bird. Every one of them advised me on how I should conduct the interrogation. With the help of the mayor, General Andreyanov, I finally managed to politely get rid of them. It was only a representative of public prosecutor's office, V. V. S., a friend of the chief prosecutor, who insisted on his presence at the interrogation.

"Well, Seryozha, you have eaten and drunk. Now, let's talk about the important stuff. Where are the stones?"

"I passed them to Misha, from the Khitrovka market."

"What scum you are, Seryozha. The likes of you always tell tall tales about the police, how they torture and beat you up. And you see how you were received by the police? We dressed you, and fed you, and as a thank-you, you're lying like a fool. What a pig you are!"

Seryozha cast down his eyes, gave it some thinking, looked at V. V. S. from under his eyelashes, and then asked me:

"Who is he?" he nodded at V. V. S.

"He is the chief prosecutor's friend."

"Mister chief," Seryozha said hesitantly, "please send him away."

Embarrassed, I turned to V. V. S. He quickly nodded, picked up his briefcase with a strained smile, and left the office.

Seryozha sighed with relief and started talking. It turned out that for more than three days, Semin had been hiding behind the icons.

When we were going through the empty space, we couldn't grope for him simply because he managed to shrink into the lower protruding part of the solid wall of icons, underneath that same step that I mentioned. When poles were put down from above, they reached the floor, but they of course couldn't penetrate steeply aside and touch the hiding man.

Through the ambush, Semin survived the torments of hunger and thirst. For the whole time he was there, he only ate a prosphoron and drank a bottle of wine that he had found in the altar. As he was trying to get out, he climbed up the wall of icons and accidentally pushed out the one that scared my agents so much when it fell down.

Semin's initial plan was to hide the jewels upon completion of the theft in a reliable place he had previously found and then get outside by breaking the window.

He intended to come back to take the stolen things after a month or two–that is, when the fuss had died down. Obviously, it would have worked exactly like that, if the laws of perspective hadn't played a bad trick on Semin.

When he was developing the plan and examining his future scene, he miscalculated the size of the window as he looked at it from below and thought it was wide enough. When he was committing the crime, however, and broke the window, he tried to fit his head through it and get outside, but the window turned out to be too narrow.

The sentry's bullet that had whistled above Semin's head alarmed him, and he started to look for a place to hide. He ran around the cathedral, saw a thick fan wire hanging by the right window and quickly climbed up the wire to the window, but then finally decided to get down and get on the floor behind the wall of icons. That's how traces of disturbed dust on the right window appeared.

"Where did you hide the things?"

"There, in the cathedral, in one of the tombs."

"Enough with the lying! We searched through all the tombs."

"You wouldn't find it; it's smartly hidden! Did you see there were two tombs next to each other under one marble cover? Between them near the floor there is a kind of an air hole in the marble, like a foot wide or so.

If you crawl through it, face down, you get between two metal coffins. Then you turn over, raise your right hand, and put it into the coffin to the right. There is an empty space between the coffin and the marble. There are the jewels, wrapped in a jacket. Didn't you notice, mister chief, that I didn't have a jacket on when I was arrested?"

"Aren't you lying, Seryozha? How come my people never found them?"

"No one could find them but me! One must really know where it is to find it."

"All right, Seryozha. Let's go to the Cathedral, and you'll get them."

Although I was afraid to use his service, because who knows what he could do there, like kill himself, I decided to take the risk. Everything went fine: Seryozha got the stolen things.

I requested that the chief prosecutor assign another investigator for this case instead of K. in order to avoid conflicts with me in the further course of the investigation. The prosecutor honored my request, and investigator Golovnya was assigned for this case. As soon as the stolen things were found, everyone started congratulating us. Metropolitan Vladimir came to thank me, and he felt embarrassed, so he ardently apologized for his doubts regarding my abilities as a detective. I ordered that the broken pieces of the Cathedral's window be made into little oval glasses, put tiny pictures of the Dormition Cathedral under them, and give them as keychain souvenirs to every person who had taken part in solving this case. And I didn't forget about investigator K., too.

Shortly, a delegation of clerical authorities visited me and gave me as a present: a copy of the icon of Vladimir Mother of God blessed by Metropolitan Vladimir in a forged silver frame with lettering on it. I gave this icon to my son, a rifleman, and it perished in Tsarskoye Selo when the Bolsheviks raided his apartment.

Semin was sentenced to eight years of hard labor. At the trial, his defender praised the Moscow Police, denouncing the rumors about how cruelly it treats criminals, and equating it with European polices (which didn't flatter me that much, actually).

At his last plea, the accused briefly stated:

"There is one thing I can tell you, gentlemen. If it hadn't been for Mr. Koshkin, you wouldn't have ever seen those diamonds again."

Those words, of course, were the best reward for me.

Victims of Pinkerton

A tall, obese man in a coat with a lambskin collar and high, lacquered boots, carrying an astrakhan hat in his hands, entered my office with a frightened face. He was around fifty, and his hair was touched with grey. He looked like a third-rate merchant. After several invitations, he finally ventured to heavily sink into the armchair, deeply sighed, and wiped his sweaty forehead.

"Who are you, and how can I help you?" I asked him.

"I am a second guild merchant, Ivan Stepanovich Artamono. I own a grocery business in Zamoskvorechye[12], but, you know, all of this doesn't matter, because it's not a merchant before you, but a dead man!"

"What do you mean, a dead man?" I was surprised.

"I mean what I said, mister chief! How am I a living man, if my death is tomorrow?"

"I don't understand at all. Would you be clearer, for God's sake?"

"I will tell you everything, mister chief. That's why I came here. You're my last hope. Save me from a disaster! Don't leave! Help me!"

The frightened merchant told me the following:

---

[12] Zamoskvorechye is an area in Moscow across the Moskva river from the Kremlin

"Yesterday, just like any other day, we shut the shop shortly past eight, let the salesmen leave, counted the day's profits, and then, since we had finished our tasks, we fired up the samovar and began to drink tea. I had three cups with my wife. She said, 'Gimme the cup, Stepanych; I'll pour some fresh tea for you.' And I said, 'No, Savishna. I don't want to drink anymore. I don't know why, but I don't feel good, like I am sick at heart or like there's a sinking feeling in the pit of my stomach.' 'It's just you ate too much okroshka[13] today,' she said. 'No, we ate just the right proportion of okroshka. That's not it, darling,' I said, 'but something's aching. Like I feel trouble.' 'Curse that tongue of yours, Stepanych!' my wife said, and she even knocked on wood. Suddenly, a bell rang. God, what the devil brought someone here at such hour?

The cook entered the dining room and handed me a letter. 'From where?' I asked.

'Some little fellow dropped by, thrust it into my hand, and went away.'

I thought it was weird. I do receive letters regarding my business, but they come in the morning and by mail, and this one came late at night and with no stamp on it.

My heart hammered. I was looking for my glasses, and I couldn't find them, even though they were right there on the table. Savishna says, 'Give it to me, honey. I'll open it and read. My eyes are younger, aren't they?' 'Please do,' I said, 'because I'm afraid!' My wife opened the envelope, and she cried, 'Jesus Christ!' I was startled and started sweating. I asked, 'What are you crying for?' 'Look, look, Stepanych!' and she held the letter out to me in her shaking hand. I took a look: Lord! Lord! Lord! Martyrdoms of earth!

At the bottom of the piece of paper, there was a spooky skeleton drawn, and a black coffin, and three candles. Take a look yourself, please!" Artamonov said, giving the letter to me.

I ran my eyes over it:

---

[13] Okroshka is Russian cold soup with vegetables, eggs, meat, and sour cream

"I command you to give me a sealed envelope with one thousand rubles in it tomorrow, on December 13, on the Swamp Square. If you disobey my command, you will be put to brutal death!

The formidable leader of a tough gang, Black Raven."

The merchant continued.

"When Savishna and I saw the skeleton and the coffin, we just sat there, the life scared out of us, and we were afraid to even read the letter. We sat like that for a while silently, and then I said, 'Well, Savishna, go ahead, read it; your eyes are keener!'

And she said, 'How come it's any of my business? You're the master, and you're the male, so you go ahead and read it!'

We argued like this, and still we were both afraid to read the letter. After everything, I called Nastya–our daughter, I mean. She's our educated girl, studies in a local school, 7th grade, but she's much too proud. Well, what can you do? 'Nastya,' I said, 'would you read this letter to us and explain step by step what it says?' Our daughter took the paper, loudly read it, shook her head and said, disgusted:

'Daddy,' she said, 'you've become the broken meat to those bloodsuckers!'

'What is that supposed to mean?' I said. 'Broken meat? I am leftovers? Scraps? We've lived our lives, we've had some gain, and we could've read this letter ourselves, you know.' I was so offended by what she had said!

She shrugged her shoulders, sniffed, and before she left, said, 'How uneducated you are, daddy. You don't understand anything!'

'You crazy fool!' I shouted in a fit of temper. 'I may be uneducated, but I did raise you, and nurtured you, and had you taught about science, and you don't even want to help your father when he's in such deadly danger!'

Well, what can I do, mister chief? It's a common thing. She doesn't respect us. So I thought, and thought again, and I decided to give up the money tomorrow. It will be too much to fork out a thousand rubles of our capital, but what can I do? I need my life more. I was so upset.

But Savishna tells me:

'It's not right what you're gonna do, Stepanych! You are a family man, and you cannot fling your money around just like that.'

'What do you mean just like that?' I said. 'My heart's bleeding like a pig, too, but what am I gonna do? I don't wanna die!'

And my wife says, 'There's gonna be no end to it. Yeah, you'll pay this one grand, and the outlaws will ask for three in a week. They'll figure you're a scared and weak merchant. So, will you pay three?'

Her words hurt, mister chief, until I was almost crying. 'No,' she says, 'Stepanych, listen to a wise woman's advice! You should go to the police, find the chief, and tell him all as it is. It's the best way! He'll protect you from the rogues, and you'll save the money.' We haggled like this until this morning, and the woman had her way. So, I came to your grace. Please, don't disregard me. Please, protect me!" Artamonov had tears in his eyes and wiped them with a handkerchief.

"Well, you should be thankful to your wife for directing you the right way. Frauds must not be encouraged! And we will protect you, but you will have to help us."

"You won't be found wanting for my help" Artamonov said, cheered up. "If there are any sort of expenses, or, if I may say, charity, we will be more than happy to—" He moved to take out his wallet.

"My friend, you must be so frightened you've lost your mind! Hide, hide your money. We don't need it. We receive salaries from the Tsar, and we are obliged to protect every single citizen from frauds.

Your assistance will be of different kind. You will have to go to the spot indicated in the letter at the indicated hour and wait for the Black Raven, and when he arrives and approaches you, you will give him an envelope stuffed with newsprint. At this moment, our people will seize him.

Artamonov almost fell off his chair.

"No way, mister chief! Spare me! Why would I beg for trouble like this? This same Raven will just shoot me down, and I'm done! I have a wife, a daughter, a business! It's not just that I don't want to meet him, but I don't even wanna see this outlaw from a mile away!

No, please, be so kind to get it all done without me somehow!"

"You are a funny man! How do we do it without you? If instead of you some other person goes, then the Black Raven will pass by without stopping, so we won't detect him and won't seize him. Besides, if he doesn't find you there, he'll get mad, and that'll put the nail in your coffin, perhaps!"

"Holy Mother! All the Saints! What do I do now? This way is bad, and the other way is even worse! Real trouble, with no way out!"

"There is a way out: Listen to me, and everything will be all right."

"How can I, mister chief, when it's so scary?!"

"What are you afraid of? Think. You will do everything the way he told you, and you will hand him the envelope. Why would he kill you or harm you?"

"Sounds right, sounds right! But what if he discovers that it's not money in the envelope, but just trash?"

"We won't give him any time to check that!"

Artamonov was deep in thought, and then he hesitantly said:

"Maybe, mister chief, you will find some daredevil who will agree to go instead of me for a reward?"

"Here we go again. The Raven knows what you look like, doesn't he? He wrote a letter to you, didn't he? He will be waiting for you, won't he?"

Finally, after lengthy persuasions, I convinced the merchant and talked him into the deal. He promised to come to the Swamp the next evening at 8:00, precisely. I sent an agent for a preliminary examination of the location's meeting. According to his report, the place was chosen by the Raven wisely, because it was a vast square. No building entrance, or a shop, or a gateway, where an ambush could be laid. I myself went to the square to take a look at it and became convinced that the report was true. But I thought it was possible to put agents in the trees that grew here and there around the square. The trees were old and branchy, so agents in them would be unnoticeable in the December twilight, lit by extremely distant kerosene streetlights.

The next day, I gave the order. About two hours before the appointed time, my ambuscaders took their places among the birds. One of them reported to me later:

"At 8 o'clock sharp, Artamonov's trembling figure appeared, and he, looking around and stumbling, began to walk around the square, keeping close to our trees. In about fifteen minutes, a boy of around 14 emerged from the side of the marketplace next to the square, approached the stupefied merchant, and roared in a feigned bass:

'The envelope!'

Artamonov, shaking with his entire body, held the envelope out and leaned back on a tree in a near-unconscious state. Without looking at it, the boy started to push the imaginary money in his bosom. And then we seized him. After searching him, we found nothing except for these three little books."

The agent put three brightly-colored copies from the Pinkerton series on my desk. One of them was titled *Black Raven*, and on the cover were a skull, crossed bones, a black coffin, and three candles.

"Well, call the Black Raven to come over here!"

A boy shedding floods of tears was brought to me.

"So you are the Black Raven, are you?"

The boy didn't answer and kept weeping.

"What a nasty boy you are! I will just order to spread you on the floor and give you half a hundred hot ones, so that you'll forget how to intimidate people with letters!"

After scolding him thoroughly, I summoned his parents. He turned out the son of a rather prosperous shopkeeper of Zamoskvorechye, as well.

His frightened parents came to the police, and when they heard about their son's escapade, they simply opened their mouths.

"That rat! That brigand! What a shame! That's why we lately started noticing money disappearing from the day's gain. Oh, we'll give him a good thrashing! That is, we'll beat him so hard, he'll remember it his entire life!"

Happy and glowing, Artamonov came again to thank for the marvelous salvation, but when he learnt what the case was, he first got angry:

"That lousy brat! Think of how much trouble he caused me!"

But he quickly calmed down, and didactically uttered:

"The reason for all this is books! Even I, mister chief, keep telling my Nastya: Stop drying your brains like this for nothing! If you're born a fool, you'll die a fool. You won't get any smarter. But can one really manage her? After reading all those ... what do you call them? Novels, she will probably elope with our salesman in charge, Saveliev!"

The Murder in Ipatievsky Lane

During the days of the sensational case about the theft in the Dormition Cathedral, another incident happened in Moscow that disturbed the people of The First Capital City[14].

The police were informed of the murder of nine people in Ipatievsky Lane.

The lane was a narrow passage paved with large cobblestone, with little houses pressed closed to each other. It was not remarkable in any way.

In one of the ramshackle buildings that should have been demolished long ago was one relatively undestroyed apartment, where a working-class family of nine huddled together. Four adult workmen and five boys constituted this family. They all came from the same village in Ryazan Province, and they worked together at a factory in Moscow.

The crime was revealed when the victims didn't show up for work. The disturbed administration sent one employee to learn the reason for the mass absence, and as he entered the ill-fated apartment, he was stunned by the blood that had leaked to the hall from underneath the doors and frozen into brown serpents. No one responded to his call. Deathlike silence reigned in the home. The administration immediately notified us, and I went straight to Ipatievsky Lane.

---

[14] The First Capital City is a literary epithet of Moscow

The old, shabby building with broken windows, warped roof, doors askew and ladders askance, resembled an abandoned beehive. No one, of course, was guarding these ruins. Naturally, there was neither a doorkeeper nor yard keepers. I went to the second floor and opened the door of the only apartment that had recently been inhabited and that was now a cemetery. Close, heavy air struck my nose, a complicated smell of a slaughterhouse, a mortuary, and a tavern. A wave of fresh air, which rushed in as I entered, started to dismally shake the cobwebs which festooned the corners of the room. This must have been the hall.

I opened the door to the right and walked in, stepping on a sticky floor entirely flooded with thickened blood. I saw two miserable beds that comprised the room's only furniture.

Two boys lay on them, one looking approximately 12, and the other 14. The two children seemed to be peacefully sleeping, and if it hadn't been for their wax-pale faces and the huge gaping wounds in the crowns of their heads, nothing would've indicated that their lives had been taken away from them. The same was in the room to the left of the hall, the only difference being that instead of two, there were three boys of approximately the same age sleeping the sleep that knows no waking. In the next room lay an adult man—apparently, a workman—with the same wound.

A corridor led from the hall straight to two adjoining rooms-- the first was big, and the one behind it was small. Two corpses of grownups lay in the big one. In the small room was a victim who showed some signs of life, so he had been taken to a hospital before I arrived. In the middle of the big room was a round table with unfinished bottles of vodka and beer on it, and near them was a piece of paper torn from a notebook. Scratched on it in broken handwriting were the words:

"Vanya and Kolya, we loved you, and we killed you."

The abundance of blood that flooded the entire apartment was striking.

Not only was the floor inundated with it, but also traces of it were everywhere: on the walls, windows, doors, and stoves.

After the search, we found a pile of ashes in the stove, in which was a half-burned collar of a male shirt, and from the very depths of the stove we retrieved a ten-pound weight that had an end with a ball on it sawed off. This missing makeshift club was, apparently, the weapon that the criminals used to fracture their victim's skulls.

There were small chests in the apartment—the usual property of a simple workman to store his simple belongings. The chests had been broken open and indicated a robbery.

I felt that the note with insane writing on it was not the end that one could grab to unravel the bloody tangle. It was, no doubt, a naïve attempt to make the investigation go down the wrong road. I am saying 'naïve,' because why would the murderers notify their dead lovers about their authorship?

Why would they risk practically leaving their calling cards?

Moreover, it seemed unlikely that two women could kill nine people so easily.

As I mentioned, the building was uninhabited, so there was no one to ask about the victims' lives or habits.

Neither was it possible to know, even roughly, the general situation, not only on the day of the murder, but also a week or a month prior to it.

I began by contacting the hospital where the surviving workman had been taken. But he was dying, unconscious, and delirious. I asked the medical staff to listen attentively to his ravings. But the result was trifling and rather odd: Among his incomprehensible ravings, the wounded man kept repeating the word 'Europe.'

Why Europe? Why did this miserable, possibly illiterate man suddenly become so fond of this part of the world?

But in a week, he died, too, and with his death, the hope to achieve the truth grew even dimmer.

In the meantime, I contacted the manufacturer to make inquiries about the dead employees. I received some interesting information, although quite vague: Some pals of the workman who had died in the hospital had heard something about the deceased man's intention to start a business with a fellow-villager of his.

Since no one had ever seen this fellow-villager, it was a very hard task to find him. However, I thought that this person, if he wasn't the key to the entire riddle, was the only chance we had to solve it.

Thus, we had to find him. I sent an agent to Ryazan Province to contact local administration and make a precise list of all the peasants from the deceased's rural district who had been living in Moscow for the previous year. There were almost 300 of them. I broke Moscow down into areas, and dozens of my agents started to interrogate natives of Ryazan who were on the list. These peasants would be questioned in detail about their lives and work in Moscow, and the name of their killed fellow-villager would be "randomly" mentioned by my agents. Of course, this approach could turn out to be like using a sledgehammer to crack a nut, but I had no other choice. I had to do it whether I wanted to or not.

A week passed without any results. Then, suddenly during the second week, when the natives of Ryazan who lived in Mary's Grove were interrogated, we found out that one of tearooms of this district had been recently sold by its old owner, a peasant from Ryazan Province named Mikhail Lyagushkin, to a new one. The tearoom was called—rather pretentiously—Europe.

Europe was a valuable find, considering the dead workman's ravings.

I started to look for Mikhail Lyagushkin. Almost everyone knew him in Mary's Grove, and everyone agreed that after selling the tearoom, he went back to his homeland, to the village, but the agent who was sent again to Ryazan Province learned that Lyagushkin never arrived.

In two weeks, a rumor started in Mary's Grove, where my people were still on watch. It was said that Lyagushkin bought a tavern in Fili, revamped it, and opened it with the same signboard, reading Europe. The information was confirmed, and Lyagushkin was immediately arrested in Fili and taken to the police. He was a tiny man with a bird-like face and shifty black eyes.

Of course, he stubbornly denied his guilt. A search conducted in Fili resulted in nothing, but detailed examination of his underwear, clothes, and footwear strengthened my suspicions, since traces of old caked blood were found in the seam between the upper and the sole of his boot. Lyagushkin said that he visited the slaughterhouse a lot. Meanwhile, chemical and microscopic analysis showed that it was human blood. Furthermore, the half-burned shirt collar found in the stove, although it was tiny, even child-sized, was just the right size for Lyagushkin.

Finally, the comparison of the handwriting on the cunning note and in the business books at Europe proved their similarity. Yet, despite the evidence, Lyagushkin kept denying everything.

We demanded that he tell us about all of his places of residence since the day of the murder until the tavern opening in Fili and received the addresses of three rooms.

Having searched them, we found nothing. But in the first apartment, the landlady told us that before moving to her place, Lyagushkin had been living for three months or so in a room in the opposite building, at a cobbler's place.

We searched the cobbler's place.

And we found valuable evidence.

In a small closet next to the room that Lyagushkin used to occupy, we found a short, sawed-off part of a weight with a ball on it. It was the piece missing from the criminal's weapon we had found in the stove.

Under the weight of new incontrovertible evidence, the criminal finally confessed.

It turned out that the killed workman had decided long ago to buy the Europe tearoom in Mary's Grove from him, and on the day of the murder, he withdrew the 5,000 rubles that he had been saving up for many years and was going to make the deed of purchase the next day. Lyagushkin stopped by his place in the evening. He had visited him many times within previous months.

The deal was celebrated in advance and drunk to. Lyagushkin treated two of the other workmen living in the same room to drinks as well.

That night, he repeatedly ran to the nearest tavern to get more.

Finally, when the hosts grew heavy with wine, he said goodbye and left, but … in an hour, he came back, went down the corridor to the big room, sneaked up to the sleeping workmen, and killed them both on the spot. Then he went to the next room and killed (to be more precise, fatally wounded) the purchaser. He stole the ill-fated 5,000 rubles from the bottom of his chest, and suddenly he was in doubt. I cite his further testimony exactly:

"No, Misha, I said to myself, don't be a fool. Finish the rest of them, too. Because they all are my fellow-villagers, the rumors will spread in the village, and they'll tell the police that such-and-such man came yesterday and drank vodka with them, so that'll put a lid on me.

Then I grabbed my stump and went back to the hall, and then to one room, and to the other two. I felt bad for smashing little children's skulls, but what could I do? Self comes first. My hand got used to the hitting, so I was cracking heads like nuts. Besides, seeing the blood was exciting: It flowed in scarlet, warm trickles down my fingers, and my heart felt somehow light and strong.

After finishing everyone else, I decided to rummage through their chests, as well, but there was only rubbish there.

By the way: I changed into a clean shirt, and burned mine, blood-stained, in the stove. And I hid the weight there, too."

It was eerie listening to the confession of this beast who told the story of his horrifying crime so calmly.

The court sentenced Lyagushkin to hard labor for life.

Marienburg Arsons

In the early 1890s, when I was the chief of the Riga Police, the Governor of Livonia, M. A. Pashkov, asked me to investigate the so-called Marienburg case.

Marienburg is a big, densely populated place in Kreis Walk that belonged to a certain Baron Wolf. The baron used to let this land on long lease, and people, as they leased it, built houses for themselves, created families, and died on it. Nothing used to break the special, peaceful lifestyle of this place–a lifestyle that nonetheless wasn't devoid of a somewhat feudal tinge. Not only was Baron Wolf the owner of the land, but he also possessed some degree of suzerain rights. Having the so-called patronage right, he nominated the local pastor, and that was exactly the initial cause of this entire case.

The new pastor the baron had appointed was out of favor with the people, and they weren't able to persuade the baron to fire him, so the protest became violent. There was a wave of arsons–first utility structures that belonged to the owner, then structures allotted to the pastor, then vast stocks of hay, bread, and other farm products that would go to the pastor, and, finally, as the arsonists got the taste of it, they switched to regular residences. Arson would be accompanied by larcenies, sometime significant ones, and there were even fatalities: An old woman and her grandson died in one of the fires.

The local police, with its small staff and modest budget, was incapable of doing anything about it. Baron Wolf sent his complaints of administrative dereliction to Petersburg, and the result was the governor's request to mobilize the Riga police force, along with an allocation of money needed for this case. Also invited to join the investigation with me was the prosecutor of the Riga court, A. N. Hesse.

Having sent a few agents ahead, I left for Marienburg with the prosecutor. Hesse wanted to familiarize himself with the way the local investigator ran the office, as the investigator was a nice person, but lacked experience. We were staying in our railcar, but spent the evening at the investigator's place. As we were going back to the train station that night, we witnessed another 'illumination.' As was later confirmed, the brazen arsonists set two huge haystacks on fire in honor of our arrival. The next day, I conducted a comprehensive investigation of the past month's fires, and I easily established the crime of arson. In some places, gunpowder wire's remains were found, in others burned tinder, and in some even traces of kerosene.

My agents spent time in taverns, beerhouses, and marketplaces, but they didn't find a single tiny hint about who could be responsible for the arsons. They only received general confirmation that the crimes were arson. Additionally, they gained the impression that, due to the month-long fuss made about this case and the local police's fruitless efforts, all of the locals were extremely cautious and restrained with any stranger. It was in vain that my agents would assure everyone that they were factory workers in a nearby town, that they had won 5,000 rubles in a German lottery (which was prohibited by our government, but nevertheless quite popular in Livonia), and that they now were looking for a business to start—a small one, but one they'd own themselves. People didn't really believe them and treated them with caution that, of course, precluded any sort of candor.

I only received material evidence of arson and rather vague information that the criminals would possibly be caught, so I came back to Riga in a rather dismal mood.

It was clear that only a native of Marienburg who enjoyed the trust of his fellow-townsmen could cast even a little light on this tough case. But we didn't have such a 'talker,' so there was only one thing I could do—create one artificially. Of course, it was going to take time, which was inconvenient, since arsons were still occurring, but lacking any other choice, I had to resort to the slow way.

I summoned one of the agents who had travelled with me and requested that he explore the ground in Marienburg to identify an appropriate sphere of business as far as he could without provoking suspicions.

Upon his return from the trip, the agent reported that our best option would be to open a beerhouse, since there were only two in that place. Besides, considering what they sell, beerhouses are always large gathering spots, which again facilitated our chances to gain the information we needed.

No sooner said than done!

I equipped two agents with counterfeit passports with stamps and residence permits for the factory where they said they had worked before winning the lottery, and I sent them to Marienburg to sell beer.

Two weeks later one of the agents came back from Riga and told me that the business was not going well: The beerhouse was always empty because people were accustomed to going to the two other beerhouses.

What was I to do?

I gave it some thought and came up with one attraction. I remembered how back in the days of my youth, I used to go to Bier-Halle in Izmailovsky Avenue, where they would always serve a salty sushka[15] with a mug of beer, so I ordered my agents to adopt the practice. One agent objected that such an expense would be a serious loss, but I agreed to the loss, so he went back to Marienburg with over a hundred pounds of salty sushkas.

The sushkas had a magical effect, and in about a week, the agents reported that the place had become very popular.

It went like this for maybe a month and a half. The New Year was coming.

My agents wrote to me:

"What should we do, sir? By the New Year, we need to renew our trade licenses, and there is a tradition that when receiving a new license, one should give an envelope with 10 or 15 rubles in it to the administration head's junior assistant and thus wish him a happy New Year."

---

[15] Sushka is a type of Russian bagel; a crunchy bread ring, often with poppy seeds on top.

I replied, "Give him the envelope and wish him a happy New Year."

So they did. One of the agents went to the administration on the appointed day, received a new license, and congratulated the assistant on the upcoming holiday by giving him a reddie[16]. Everything went smoothly.

In the meantime, the arsons were still occurring. I was nervous and hurried my 'businessmen.'

Finally, in early February, they reported that they had strong suspicions regarding certain persons who visited their beerhouse. This gang, consisting of a blacksmith and two sons of the church watchman, was headed by a certain Zalit, the local chief fireman and photographer. The suspicions were based, first of all, on the fact that according to the residents of the town, all of these people, especially the watchman's sons, had been paupers before. And yet, within the past few months, they would fling their money about and spend whole days in the beerhouse drinking incredible amounts of beer. Furthermore, there was a story that the blacksmith had gotten drunk and blabbed. He predicted there would be a fire that night and dropped a hint at which building was doomed. The prediction came true, and the building was burned down. Agents immediately gave us the addresses of those four persons under suspicion.

With this detailed information, I left for Marienburg, accompanied by A. N. Hesse and a few of my people.

We reached the spot in the evening, waited for the night, then left our car, broke into three groups, and simultaneously attacked the chief fireman, the blacksmith, and the watchman's sons.

The victory was total.

At Zalit's place, as well as at the places of his accomplices, we found significant amounts of money, the origin of which they couldn't explain. We also found at each place wax envelopes with

---

[16] Bills were commonly referred to by their colors. Reddie is the ten-ruble bill.

gunpowder wires, dozens of feet of tinder, large stocks of kerosene, etc.

They all, of course, were arrested and taken to Riga.

I attended the much-talked-of trial of these arsonists in Riga, and I had a rather odd conflict with the defender, the famous Petrograd lawyer G. As a witness, I told the judges frankly and in detail about the beer trick that I had to resort to in order to find the criminals. The presiding judge, as is usual, asked the prosecutor and the defender if they had questions for the witness. The prosecutor's answer was negative, but the attorney at law G. said quick-temperedly:

"Oh, yes! I do!" He turned to me and asked in a brazen and sarcastic tone, "Please tell me, curious witness, was there any more scheming of yours in Marienburg?"

I addressed the judge:

"Your Honor, I ask you to kindly protect me from the attacks of this bumptious gentleman!"

The judge took my side and said to G.:

"Mister G., I call you to order and ask you to ask questions for the witness through me and have them more decently formulated!"

G. objected:

"I request to incorporate the witness's words addressed to me in the record."

I requested the same.

"Do you have any other questions?" the judge asked G.

"No, I do not."

Thus the incident was over.

Zalit, the chief fireman, was sentenced to eight years of hard labor.

His accomplices, I think, got off with lesser sentences.

Upon the completion of the case, I called the administration head's assistant and had a talk with him in the presence of my agent.

"Listen, you're going to have to give the reddie back! That was public money."

He was very embarrassed.

"Yes, sir!" He hastily dipped his fingers into his wallet.

Sweaty, red as a crayfish, he begged me for a very long time to not report the governor on this shameful thing he had done, and I was so glad about the success of the case that, I confess, I preferred to forget about this guy.

Dactylography

Dactylography repeatedly did me a good turn in combating the criminal world. One case was especially engraved on my memory.

But before I tell about it, I have to digress and remind the reader, in general terms at least, what dactylography is. There are no two people in the world with identical prints on the skin of their fingers. The difference is in the skin spirals, or serifs, or wrinkles— but there is always a difference, without fail. This special aspect of the skin is very reliable. Thus no burns or other injuries of cutaneous covering are able to transform the original print. The burn will pass, the injury will skin over, and again the same print that has been on it since the person was born will appear on the newly born skin. Modern dactylographic systems are based on this curious natural feature that has been known since ancient times. In Moscow, I developed and applied the first relatively fast method of finding fingerprints identical with freshly taken ones among numerous previously taken ones. It proved successful and was shortly employed in England, where the English police still use it.

So, in 1910, I was notified on the telephone that the body of a man around 45 years old, murdered with a dagger stabbed into his chest, was found in a first-class compartment of a train that had just arrived from Rostov.

Accompanied by coroner C. and police doctor M., I immediately went to the Kursky railway terminal. The car with the murdered man in it was detached and placed on one of the siding lines.

We opened the compartment's door and saw the following: Lying on the lower sofa, his head turned to the window, was a man of around 45 wearing a jacket without a collar (it was on a net shelf on the wall near him). His right hand hung down, fingers touching the floor. Sticking out from the left part of the dead man's chest was the white ivory handle of a dagger stabbed deep into his body.

The corpse's face was peaceful. He looked like a tranquilly sleeping man, which made me think that he had been instantly killed, probably in his sleep. Anyway, there were no traces of struggle. Everything was in order in the compartment: Two locked suitcases lay on the top shelf, and an open box of Tula gingerbread[17] was on the table, which seemed to imply that the murder probably had taken place between Tula and Moscow.

After searching the dead man, we found a new wallet, monogrammed with the letter 'K' and containing 275 rubles, in the side pocket of his jacket. In the left pocket of his pants was a wrinkled, but never used, handkerchief with a big red mark (also 'K'), and in the right pocket, a smooth silver cigar case with a big gold monogrammed 'K' and two gold ornaments: a naked woman and a little cat with tiny emeralds instead of the eyes. The cigar case especially drew my attention, so I began to scrutinize it, carefully holding it by the ribs with my fingers.

I noticed two small blood stains and traces of a grip. I immediately examined the murdered man's hands, but it turned out they were clean, without the slightest traces of blood on them. I couldn't help thinking the cigar case was slipped to the murdered man by the murderer after the crime was committed.

Due to the fact that the valuable things like the watch (which the murdered man had), the wallet with 275 rubles in it, and others, were untouched, it looked like the aim of the crime wasn't robbery.

The dead man had no identification documents. We interrogated the conductor, whose shift started in Oryol, and we learnt that the last time he had seen the deceased was in Tula, when the latter was going back to his car with a box of gingerbread in his hands. The murder was only discovered upon the train's arrival to Moscow, at the regular round made by a sub-officer of gendarmerie. I ordered the

---

[17] Tula gingerbread is a type of Russian gingerbread with an imprint on top and jam, honey, or condensed milk inside. It is traditionally produced in the city of Tula about 200 km from Moscow

corpse transferred to a hospital ward, took a copy of the inspection record and the murdered man's things, and went back to my office. I was carrying the cigar case with extreme care.

When I came down to the detective police, I immediately summoned the functionary who was a specialist in dactylography and requested that he decode the fingerprints on the cigar case. He carefully poured some special, incredibly fine and dry powder on the gripped surface, then carefully blew it off, and a thin layer of the powder remained stuck to the slightly greasy metal surface without leaving a trace on the areas where the skin spiral curls showed up. It was sort of a black field dug through with spiral-like trenches. The print was immediately photographed and processed in a particular formula, and after that we filed it with a group of properly registered cards.

It turned out to be a new one, i.e., one we didn't have in our collection. Therefore, the criminal wasn't a professional or a recidivist.

This case didn't captivate me, since in the beginning it appeared quite banal to me. There were no signs of robbery, which meant that the criminal was guided by the motive of revenge.

I thought we should identify the victim, after which the crime would be easily solved. I was only somewhat confused by the cigar case that seemed to have been slipped to the victim by the murderer. But many times in my practice, I had seen such tricks aimed at making the investigation go down the wrong road.

I posted a message in all the newspapers of Moscow about a dead body on a train from Rostov, about the way he looked, and about the cigar case that he had with him with the monogram 'K' and with the ornaments of a woman and a cat with emerald eyes. I was sure that the next day the murdered man's friends or family would come to see me. Indeed, the next day, at around noon, I was informed that a lady wished to see me concerning this case.

"Let her in," I said to the courier.

A rather young lady with a worried face and tearful eyes entered my office.

"I came to you after I read in the newspapers, about finding the dead body of—alas!—I am afraid, my poor husband!" the lady started crying.

I tried to calm her down.

"What makes you think that the murdered man is your husband, madam?"

"You see, about a week ago my husband went to Rostov on business, and he was supposed to come back yesterday. But he didn't, and he didn't inform me on the reason of his delay, which doesn't seem like him at all. And your description fits him, and, mainly, the cigar case ... I don't even know what to think about this cigar case. According to the description, it's my husband's case exactly, but, on the other hand, a week before his departure my husband had lost it, and was very saddened by the loss, for he valued this memorable gift of mine. How it got back to his pocket, I cannot even imagine. But, regardless, I am very, very worried."

I took the ill-fated cigar case from a drawer and held it out to her.

As soon as she saw it, the lady gave a cry:

"That's it! That's Mitya's case! I even know that inside it, on the gilded surface, in the corner, there is my name scratched, 'Vera.'"

Indeed, what she said was true, so there was no doubt left.

"Tell me, madam, did someone steal this cigar case from your husband, say, a week before? Didn't you suspect anyone?"

"No, my husband flatly insisted that he had lost it somewhere in the street after putting it in the torn pocket of his coat."

"And yet, you see, it's not lost."

"I don't know what to think! Will you allow me to go and see the deceased?"

"Of course, madam. I will give you one of the agents to accompany you; please, go."

We parted. "Poor woman," I thought. "You are so unlikely to escape the bitter cup of widowhood." And how surprised was I when in about an hour and a half she entered my office again, shining with joy and happiness.

"Imagine my happiness! The murdered man is not my husband at all! Oh, Lord, You have mercy on me! I am revived now, like I was born again. I am happy, sir, as I haven't been for a long time!"

"Well, congratulations! I am very, very glad for you! But yet I ask you to send your husband to me immediately upon his return from Rostov."

"Of course, I will send him without fail."

"Concerning the cigar case, I need to keep it for now, but upon completion of the case, I hope, I will be able to give it back to you. Goodbye, madam."

We thus said goodbye to each other and parted.

In the evening of the same day a person named Strindman, a co-owner of a jewelry store near Kuznetsky Most, came to see me and told me that something was worrying him. His business partner, Ozolin, according to the latter's telegram, was supposed to come back from Rostov on the previous day. The goal of his trip was to purchase a diamond necklace from a lady he knew. Both store co-owners were well familiar with this necklace, since last year they had already raised the question of the purchase, but back then they didn't agree on the price. Now the necklace's owner had offered to sell it to them again and had exchanged letters with Ozolin. He left for Rostov to settle the bargain. Although Strindman read in the newspapers that the dead man's things had the monogram 'K' on them, he still decided to ask me if he might take a look at the body. I gave my permission, of course, and the murdered man turned out to be Ozolin.

So, the case unexpectedly got a new twist. The criminal wasn't guided by revenge, but mercenary motives. Even when I was examining the body at the crime scene, an assumption crossed my mind that the cigar case was slipped as a blind. Now the assumption transformed into a certainty, and, moreover, the new wallet with 275 rubles and a handkerchief, apparently, were put there deliberately by the criminal too.

"Tell me," I asked Strindman. "How much do you think the necklace costs?"

"We paid 58,000 for it."

"Except for you, did anyone else know about the aim of the deceased's trip?"

"No-one did, except for our salesman Aaronov."

"Could he commit the murder?"

"Oh, no, sir! We have known Yasha for a very long time, since he was a child. He is an honest boy. Besides, he has been working nonstop the entire time, and by this reason alone, he couldn't commit this crime."

"Tell me, do you suspect anyone at all?"

"Positively no one! I don't know what to think about all this!"

I thought for a little while and then said:

"You see, for the sake of the investigation I cannot neglect anything. Pardon me, but I have to ask you, for the sake of my conscience, to put your finger down, too."

"What do you mean 'put my finger down'?"

"You'll see now."

I summoned the functionary, and he performed the dactylographic procedure on Strindman. The fingerprint we received didn't help us.

"Have you ever seen the deceased with this cigar case?" I held it out to him.

He took a good look at the cigar case and shook his head:

"No, never! Besides, the deceased didn't smoke."

"Very good. I will send an agent with you who will accompany you to your store and bring Aaronov back to me."

In two hours or so I was interrogating Aaronov, a young man of around 20, quite shy and very frightened. He didn't tell me anything new, but only confirmed that he knew the reason why Ozolin had traveled to Rostov.

Asked if he had ever told anybody about it, Aaronov replied negatively. His fingerprint didn't match with the fingerprints on the cigar case. I let him go.

The case was not getting clearer, and, most importantly, I couldn't find a thread that I could catch to lead the investigation further towards success.

We notified, of course, all the jewelers in Moscow and Petrograd about the stolen necklace and gave the detailed description provided by Strindman. However, I didn't think it was so important because, first of all, the murderer and thief could have taken the stones out of their sockets and sold them one by one, and, second, which was more probable, could have refrained from getting rid of the stolen things for a while or have dealt it in through an unscrupulous person he knew.

Three or four days went like this, without any results. During this time, happy Vera's 'missing' husband came back and visited me. His testimony, however, didn't add anything new to the investigation, and his fingerprint, of course, confirmed his innocence.

Many times in my detective practice, I noticed that one shouldn't neglect certain methods of finding the criminal even when the chances of success behind those methods seem trifling. Sometimes the most incredible maneuvers would unexpectedly benefit me. In this obscure case, I didn't seem to have a choice, so I resorted to an unlikely ruse that nevertheless turned out to be very effective.

I posted an announcement in all of the newspapers in Moscow with the following content: "1,000 ruble reward to the person who returns or indicates the location of a lost silver cigar case with a gold K monogram and gold ornaments of a nude woman and a cat with emerald eyes. For credibility, provide a detailed description of cigar case and its secret features when indicating its locality.

The case holds extreme sentimental value.

4 Nikolo-Peskovky Lane, apartment 2, inquire actress Vera Alexandrovna Neznamova."

Clearly, the actress Neznamova and her accompanist who rehearsed with her all the time, as well as a quite shabby footman, were my agents. The apartment in 4 Nikolo-Peskovky Lane belonged to one of my subordinates.

Of course, I didn't hope that the murderer would jump at this crude bait, but I thought that maybe 1,000 rubles might tempt one of the minor accomplices, if there were any.

The day after the announcement was published, my agent ran into my office and cheerfully reported:

"I think we have brought the murderer!"

"Really? The murderer? Calm down, please, and tell me what happened."

"So, sir, we were in the apartment, cooling our feet. The moment I heard any noise in the staircase, I would immediately dash to the piano to ferociously yell scales, and my accompanist would sing along with me.

All of yesterday was like this. And we did the same thing this morning. But about an hour ago, someone suddenly rang the doorbell. Silantiev put a napkin over his arm and went to answer the door, while Ivanov and I started singing something like 'May my prayer be set before you' or 'Do not tempt me without reason.' A young man, around 18 years old, entered the room and looked at me inquiringly. I said languishingly to Ivanov:

'Excuse me, maestro.'

'Please, please!' he said and left the room.

Then I said to the visitor:

'How can I help you, monsieur?'

'Tell me, please, are you Mrs. Neznamova?'

'Yes.'

'Did you post an ad in the newspapers about a cigar case?'

'Yes, I did. Why? Do you have it?' I said, simulating excitement.

'Well, maybe I don't have it with me, but I can tell you exactly where it is.'

I pouted with disappointment:

'Yes, it's wonderful, of course, but, but ... why should I believe you?'

'Well, because I will describe it in the most precise manner, and you will see that there's no doubt I'm talking about your dear souvenir.'

So he described the case to me in the most detailed way, and he didn't forget, of course, to mention the name 'Vera' scratched on the inside lid.

'Yes, no doubt you're talking about my cigar case. Where is it now?'

'Ooh, madam, who does it like that? Money first.'

'Maestro!' I shouted.

The accompanist and the footman entered the room with Brownings in their hands. I pointed at the badly frightened young man and said:

'Take him, gentlemen!'

He was taken away in handcuffs and brought here. He said his name was Simon Shmuelevitz, a Russian Orthodox Christian and an apprentice to the watchmaker Fyodorov, whose shop is on Vozdvizhenka Street."

"Thank you for the well-accomplished assignment. Now please send this Shmuelevitz person to me."

A young man trembling with fear entered the office and stopped, perplexed, in the middle of the room.

"So, Simon, got into a pretty mess here, huh, pal?"

Shmuelevitz jumped up as if spring-mounted and started talking really, really fast:

"Oh, mister chief, Your Excellency, for God's sake, let me go, 'cause I am as innocent as a lamb. I am a poor, humble Christian who doesn't mean harm to anyone. Well, I did want to have a small deal there (Shmuelevitz screwed up his eyes and rounded his fingers to show how small the deal was). But what would be wrong about that? The madam promised 1,000 rubles in a newspaper. I wanted to earn it fairly."

"It's all a beautiful story, but the cigar case that you described so precisely for some reason was found on a murdered man. So, how could you know even about the name 'Vera' on the lid? It looks like perhaps it was you who killed that man."

Shmuelevitz jumped up as if stung and started to squeak hysterically:

"Oh, please, don't even say that, chief, sir! How could I?! How can you say that! To kill a man?! Oh, my God! Simon believes in God and is incapable of doing that. I will tell you everything, tell you as it is, and won't lie even a little bit!"

"Go ahead. Tell me."

Shmuelevitz, breathless with hastiness, started talking with emphatic gesticulation:

"One morning, sir, I read in a newspaper about a person murdered on a train from Rostov, and when I reached the part about the cigar case, I at once felt a pang of fear in my stomach. Because a cigar case exactly like that was bought by my master for 24 rubles from some soldier who stopped by our shop, just a week before that. I really liked that cigar case, so I would take good looks at it. In a couple of days it was gone. My master had taken it somewhere. Then, suddenly, yesterday I read that lady's ad, and I thought: Look alive, Simon. You can make some good money here.

And the money is really good, a thousand rubles! Oh, it even made my head whizz. Right, the case was found on a killed man, but it really wasn't my fault! I was going to frankly tell this lady that the case was with the police, and she would pay me the whole 1,000 rubles. And that'd be it. I am an honest person, mister chief!"

His story sounded true. But I still ordered to lift Shmuelevitz's fingerprints. Although it didn't help us, I thought it necessary to detain him temporarily.

Two agents were immediately sent to get Fyodorov the watchmaker, and an hour later, he was before me. He was a tall man of typical Russian appearance, with a wide, quite pretty face, but somewhat unpleasant expression of his shifty eyes.

He was rather calm and told me that indeed he had purchased the cigar case from a soldier more than a week ago, and in a day, he had sold it to a random unknown customer. I couldn't get any more from him, so I was going to let him go, but before, again for the sake of my conscience, I ordered the dactylographic print of his fingers. I was dismal, sitting in my office, trying to invent some new approach to this case that I just didn't seem able to figure out, when suddenly the functionary entered with two prints, the murderer's and Fyodorov's, and excitedly told me that they matched. I carefully scrutinized both prints. No doubt: Ozolin's murderer was found.

Another two-hours-long interrogation of Fyodorov, even with the presentation of considerable evidence, didn't make him confess or tell where the stolen things were. Apparently, he didn't believe in the dactylographic method and thus didn't understand the heaviness of this conclusive evidence.

I summoned Shmuelevitz again.

"Here's the deal, Simon, your master turned out a murderer, so his affair is settled. He won't get away from a hard labor sentence. He can draw you into this case, too, because you did see the cigar case, and you did go there to get the 1,000 rubles, and so on. So the best you can do is not to conceal anything and answer my questions frankly. Otherwise, I repeat, he'll send you to prison."

"Please ask, mister chief. I won't hide anything. Why would I hide anything? I am innocent, and concealing a murderer is not something Simon would do. I am ready for everything, everything, mister chief!"

"Great! So tell me please, how long have you been working for Fyodorov?"

"More than three years, mister chief."

"Whom did he keep up acquaintance with? Whom did he visit?"

"He's not a rich man. His business wasn't going well, so none of his friends would visit him. Neither would he go anywhere to visit, aside from his mother."

"Where does his mother live?"

"In the suburbs, behind the Dragomilovskaya Zastava Square."

"How often would he visit her?"

"Not too often, once a week, maybe."

"How do you know that? Did he tell you where he was going to?"

"Yes, Master often told me, and he also took me with him a few times."

"Tell me, within past two weeks did your master leave the shop for a long while?"

Shmuelevitz hesitated a bit, and then resolutely said:

"He did, mister chief, in fact he really did."

"When exactly?" I asked.

"Something like six or seven days ago, he was out for quite a while."

"Try to remember the day exactly."

Shmuelevitz rolled up his eyes, rubbed his forehead, and then remembered. Hesaid:

"Yes, yes! It was last Tuesday! (The day the corpse was found.) On Monday, he closed the shop and left, and then came back

120

on Tuesday at around 3 in the afternoon. He took a rest for four hours, and then in the evening left again and came back that night."

"Where did he go?"

"The first time, I don't know, and the second time, I bet, he went to his mother."

"What makes you think that?"

"Because there's this impassible haze all around the place behind the Zastava Square, so Master always comes back cursing, all dirty. And it was like this on Tuesday night, too."

"Here's the deal, Simon: Your master will be sent to hard labor, his shop will be closed, and you'll lose your job, unless, of course, you yourself will be brought before the court. So that's what I offer: I will give you 100 rubles, and if you accomplish the mission I assign for you, I will find a job for you in some other watchmaker's place. But, of course, you're going to have to help us for this."

"Why would I refuse the offer to earn 100 rubles?"

"There you go! Not only did your master kill a man, but also stole a diamond necklace from him, and apparently he hid it at his mother's place, behind the Dragomilovskaya Zastava Square. We need to find it. Of course, I'll order to search the shop, but I am quite sure it's not there."

"Of course it's not! The diamonds must be at his mother's place," Shmuelevitz said with certainty.

"I don't want to conduct a search there, because a house in the suburbs definitely comes with a big yard and a kitchen garden. A mother and son could bury the stones anywhere, and one really cannot dig over an entire estate!"

"No, one cannot, mister chief."

"So, I came up with the following idea: They do know you well, don't they?"

"They really do. I am like family!"

"Wonderful! So tonight you'll run to her place, breathless, give her a little bundle of fake jewels, and whisper to her in a frightened voice, 'Master told me to give this bundle to you and asked you to hide it as soon as possible in the same place where he hid the diamonds. The police is watching him, so he didn't want to come here and sent me instead.' After this you'll shove the bundle in her hands and run back here without looking back. Do you think you can carry this all out?"

"Why not? I'll do it, mister chief."

I sent agents to jewelry stores, and in about an hour they got me two dozen 'jewels': earrings, rings with colorful fake stones, thick chains and strings, etc.

Shmuelevitz tied them up into his dirty handkerchief and rushed to the Dragomilovskaya Zastava Square, followed from a distance by my able and experienced agent Muratov. I had much to do, so I didn't notice how time passed. At around 9 in the evening, Shmuelevitz came to me, shining, and said:

"Oh, mister chief! I did it all just the way you told me."

"Tell me in detail."

"What do I tell? The mother got all fussy, gasped, and promised to do everything precisely the way her son told her. She quickly hid the bundle in her pocket, and I ran back."

"Well done, Simon! Now take what I promised." I held out the hundred-ruble bill I promised to Shmuelevitz.

In the morning, Muratov came to my office and solemnly put a string of large diamonds with a beautiful antique clasp on my desk.

"So, Muratov, how did it go?"

"It was very easy, sir. Right after Shmuelevitz left, I took up a position for surveillance by hiding behind a fence that goes around the yard and the house. I had to stay there for quite a long time, until I thought that maybe she had decided to hide the things inside the house. Then suddenly, a little past ten, the mother went out to the porch, looked around, then went across the yard to a shed, grabbed a shovel, and dragged herself along to the very end of the yard, toward

122

the well. It was a moonlit night, so I could see everything as if in the daylight. She started to dig behind the well, dug up a tin cookie box, put Shmuelevitz's bundle into it, buried it back in the same place, leveled off the ground, threw some trash on it, put the shovel back in the shed, and went back home. Early in the morning, at dawn, I came to her with a warrant for her arrest and demanded that she gave the necklace up.

But she was stubborn and kept saying, 'I know nothing. There's nothing I know.'

Then we went to the well, dug up the hidden things where I indicated, and drew up the record. The women acted very surprised and kept denying everything."

"You fulfilled the assignment brilliantly, Muratov. Thank you very much!"

My agent bowed.

I ordered to bring arrested Fyodorov.

"Here's the thing, my dear friend," I said in a severe tone, "if you keep denying everything even now and don't tell me the truth, I will send both of you to Siberia, you and your mother who buried these diamonds (I pointed at the stones on the desk) in her yard near the well behind the Dragomilovskaya Zastava. So you might as well be frank. Although, you might not, and that's just as well. It's up to you," I lazily yawned and looked at the clock. "So?" I asked after a pause.

Fyodorov puffed, thought for a while, shifted from foot to foot for a couple of times, then resolutely shook his head, and spoke rapidly:

"Well, since you have the stones now, I guess that's it! It's over."

"Tell me how you killed him and who assisted you."

"No one assisted me. I did it by myself. I thought I'd finally make my way, but now even that failed! My watchmaker business didn't go well, I could barely make ends meet, I led a poor life, and I wanted to live like a decent man, so here's where the devil's work was.

I met Aaronov, whom I knew before, on Tverskoy Boulevard. He works for Strindman and Ozolin near Kuznetsky Most. We talked. So Aaronov started bragging that his master, according to him, had a huge business, running into millions. And I said to him that he was lying, because it was just a shop that they had, just a trifling shop and nothing more. And he said, 'How trifling is it that Ozolin sent a telegram yesterday that he would come tomorrow from Rostov with a purchase? Do you know what that purchase is? A diamond necklace worth 58,000 rubles! Does this sound like a trifling shop now?' This conversation really sank into my mind. This was a real opportunity to get rich. All I needed to do is think it through and do everything right. Right there, on the Boulevard, I started to develop a plan. If I didn't take any of the valuable things from Ozolin except for the necklace, no one would think it was a robbery. And in order for the murdered man to not be identified, I would disorient the police by slipping fake marks. I chose the letter 'K' because I had the silver monogrammed cigar case I had just bought, so I got a handkerchief and a wallet with the same letter on them. By the way, I needed the wallet to exchange it with the murdered, too, because he might have some big money with him, and leaving him without a wallet at all was impossible, because that would look like a murder for mercenary motives. I remember I asked Aaronov if Ozolin was afraid to have such valuable things with him during his travel. And he said, 'Why would he be afraid? Ozolin will take a small single compartment on the Rostov train, and he will be there alone, so who could possibly steal from him?'

That same night I went to Tula, where I decided to wait for the train to Moscow. I well knew Ozolin by sight. He really was on that train, and in Tula, he left the first-class car, bought a box of gingerbread in one of the stands, then walked a little bit along the platform, and went back to his car. I went to that same car, too. Ozolin's compartment was third. After we were about 50 miles past Tula, I picked a moment, came up to Ozolin's compartment, turned the lock with a railway key I prepared beforehand, and slowly, carefully opened the door. Ozolin was lying on his back, deep in his sleep, quietly snoring. I silently went in and killed him on the spot with a bad blow of a dagger. He didn't cry out; he didn't even move. After that, I quickly closed the door, locked it, and started looking for the necklace. It turned out it was in the inset pocket of his vest. I snatched his wallet and slipped him mine, prepared in advance, with

275 rubles in it. I shoved the handkerchief in one of the pockets of his pants, and the cigar case in the other one, then I went to the corridor, locked his door, and quickly went to the restroom. There wasn't much in his wallet—like 400 or so rubles. I put them into my pocket and flushed the wallet down the closet.

After that I took a good shower and went back to my compartment. In Moscow, I left the train and walked home. What happened then—I do not know. I told you the truth."

The court sentenced Fyodorov to eight years of hard labor for premeditated murder.

I wanted to keep my word, so I intended to find a job for Simon in some watchmaker's shop, but Shmuelevitz suddenly got a taste for being a detective, so he asked me to stay at the police, and I let him. Afterwards, he made a pretty competent agent, although not a big one, whose field was searching for missing cats and dogs.

"Chief of the Department of Security"

Schwabo, the inspector of the Sokolniki District, reported to me:

"Sir, today I learned something rather odd in Sokolniki. I stopped by the Vienna tavern to chat with the owner, which I often do, because he likes to talk and once in a while he provides me with information. And indeed, today he told me a curious story. A certain person named Ivan Prokhorov Borodin often comes to the tavern. He's around fifty, a local rich man, the owner of a brick factory. Ivan Prokhorov is a big deal in Sokolniki. The tavern-keeper appreciates an acquaintance with him and even seems proud of it. However, the day before yesterday, an unpleasant and strange accident happened to this Ivan Prokhorov person. He was in the Vienna, peacefully drinking tea with the owner. Suddenly a car pulled over, and a gendarmerie officer got out, along with two lower officers and a man in civilian clothes.

They entered the tavern, arrested Borodin and took him to an unknown destination without any explanation. However, within 24 hours, yesterday that is, Borodin showed up in the tavern again, very depressed, and told the tavern keeper in confidence that the gendarmes took him to the Department of Security, searched him, threatened him with banishment from Moscow, took away an annuity bill worth 5,000 rubles from him and let him go until tomorrow under the condition that he would bring another 5,000 rubles to their office. Otherwise, his arrest and deportation to Narym Krai would be inevitable. Ivan Prokhorov is badly scared, so is going to give them the 5,000 rubles tomorrow just in order to stay safe. The tavern keeper described his intense fright and obedience—people say Ivan Prokhorov's past isn't particularly clean. Rumor has it that his wealth comes from 'Guslitsy money.'"

The expression "Guslitsy money" was quite famous. About 25-30 years prior, there was a much-discussed case of a gang of counterfeiters who produced fake banknotes in the village of Guslitsy, not far from Moscow.

I ordered Schwabo to immediately go to Borodin and calmly invite him for a talk with the Chief of Police.

I do not know precisely how Schwabo carried out my order, but I guess it wasn't diplomatic, judging by what Schwabo said when he brought Borodin to the police department three hours later. He came into my office to report the completion of the order.

"When I informed Borodin about your offer for him to talk with you, sir, he was terrified. 'My God!' he exclaimed, 'What is that? Yesterday the Chief of the Department of Security, and today the Chief of Police? One just can't have that much money!' But then he came to his senses, quickly got dressed, and followed me without saying a word more."

"Let him in, please!"

A tall, solidly built man entered my office. He had a handsome face, and his beard and temples were grayish. His face was somewhat petrified, indicating either misery or anxiety being diligently hidden.

"Sit down, please!" I said in as friendly a voice as possible.

"Thank you very much," he said and slowly sat down.

"Tell me, please, what was that odd story that happened to you? Why were 5,000 rubles taken away from you, and why is the same amount about to be taken away from you again?"

"What 5,000?" Borodin asked, pretending to be surprised. "I have no idea what you are talking about! There was no five thousand taken away from me. In fact, I am not complaining about anything, and I am content with everything, very much."

"Enough of that kind of talk, Ivan Prokhorovich! I have summoned you for your own good. It's clear that you've faced frauds and they managed to intimidate you, so that's why you're denying everything. If you had been arrested by real gendarmes, you wouldn't have been released so soon, and they wouldn't have been extorting money from you. Think for a moment, think hard, and tell me everything. I wish nothing but the best for you."

As I was saying this, my visitor's face was turning from pale-yellow to crimson, and little beads of sweat appeared on his forehead. He started panting, then suddenly cracked his knuckles, and burst into agitated, rapid talking:

"You are right, sir. Why would I hide anything from you?

I smelled the rat in this whole thing, too.

If you can, please protect me. I beg you, in the name of Christ, please do not give me up. I will tell you everything. I'll tell you absolutely everything! Yesterday, I was arrested by a gendarmerie officer with two soldiers and one civilian. They put me in their car and took me to Skatertny Lane, to the place that I was told was the Department of Security.

I do not remember the address, but I would recognize the building. We went to the third floor. There I was immediately searched, and they took my wallet away. There was a 5,000 annuity bill and 300 rubles of cash. The wallet with the money in it was then tied up with laces and sealed. Then I was taken to the hall and told, 'Wait here. The chief is busy now.' So I sat there for half an hour, and for another half an hour. A person in handcuffs was escorted past me, then two gendarmerie sub-officers passed by. Finally, a gendarme came and accompanied me to the chief's office.

I entered: It was a big room. In the middle was a desk with papers piled up on it and a man in civvies sitting at it. I stopped. He didn't even look at me and kept writing quickly. Ten minutes or so passed like this. A gendarmerie officer entered, put a big briefcase on the desk, and handed papers to the chief. The chief scanned through it and said, 'I'll make arrangements.' Then he took the phone receiver, said some number. 'Is that you, Saveliev? It's the Chief of the Department of Security speaking. Get your people and immediately arrest Petrovsky, now!' Finally he raised his head and told me, 'So that's what you're like, rogue! We've been watching you and looking into your past for quite a while now. But enough is enough. You've had your share of freedom. Sending you behind bars is long overdue.'

'Please, mister chief,' I begged, 'Why me? Thank God, I lead a humble, good life, harming no-one. Why would you send me behind bars?'

'Stop acting like a fool and playing innocent!' he cried to me. 'Have you forgotten your Guslitsy affairs?'

I was simply stupefied."

"What are those 'Guslitsy affairs'?" I asked Borodin in the most innocent voice.

"Well, there's nothing to hide, sir! It happened about 25 years ago. I was just a boy tricked by counterfeiters who produced fake money in Guslitsy. I did my time for that, and since then, I have been living an honest life.

And when the Guslitsy money was brought up, I thought that things were rotten! The chief ordered to bring my wallet, broke the seal, took the money out of it and said:

'There was quite a lot of Guslitsy money that wound up in your hands, but the hell with it! We have a charity drive currently, so we need money, but we don't have any. So I offer you the following: I will release you till the day after tomorrow on this 5,000 as a bail, and you have to bring 5,000 to this same place the day after tomorrow by two o'clock. If you do, I'll let you go to the wind, and if you don't—it will be you alone to blame. You will be immediately arrested, banished from Moscow, and within 24 hours sent to Narym Krai to milk seals.'

After saying this, the chief released me, but kept the annuity and the three one hundred rubles-bills."

"Here's the deal!" I said to Borodin. "Go to Skatertny Lane with my agent and point at the building where you were, and tomorrow at eleven come back to me."

Borodin showed the building, and we asked the yard keepers about the tenants of the third floor. They were described as humble people provoking no suspicions. We also learned the phone number of the apartment. But what were we to do next? I didn't want to conduct an unexpected search because the frauds might happen not to be home.

The money they had taken from Borodin might be taken away from the apartment too. Besides, Borodin didn't remember the number of his bill. Therefore, even if the swindlers were seized, they could deny everything, the more so because there had been no witnesses. That is why I stuck to the third plan. Surveillance was set up for the building and the apartment on the third floor especially. I waited for Borodin to come to me the next day.

In several hours, after surveillance was set up, one of the agents came running to me and reported that Vasily Gilevich walked out of the apartment on the third floor. We were familiar with him after a series of petty frauds.

Vasily was the brother of Andrei Gilevich, student Prilutsky's killer. I described this case in one of the previous short stories. Obviously, Borodin was blackmailed by this "reputable" representative of the "reputable" family.

I invited a stenographer and a yard keeper to my office as future witnesses and gave them branch receivers of my telephone. When Borodin came, I talked to him for about 10 minutes, trying to catch the manner he spoke, his locution, his intonations, etc. After that I told him to sit still and listen.

The stenographer, sitting by one of the branch receivers, prepared a sheet of paper and several pencils; the yard keeper took the branch receiver delicately with his fingers. When everything was ready, I lifted my receiver.

"Miss, number so-and-so, please!"

"You're on!"

I heard a female voice.

"I'm listening."

"Can I speak with mister chief, please?"

"Yes, just a minute."

Shortly, I heard a male voice.

"Hello, I'm listening!"

"Is that you, mister chief?"

"Hm. Who's speaking?"

"It's Ivan Prokhorov Borodin. You ordered me to come to see you today."

"So, swindler, you got the money?"

"Please don't be mad, mister chief. I swear, there's no way I can get it by two o'clock, but I was promised I'll get it by four. So that's why I'm calling. Would you kindly allow me to be two hours late. There's no way I can make it sooner! Five thousand rubles are a whole year's capital, and it's hard to gather that much at once!"

"You butterfingers! You sleepy head! Well, what the hell, take your time. But remember that if you do not come at four, you'll be gone from Moscow within 24 hours like a shot from a gun." Then, with some anxiety, he continued, "How did you know my phone number? Do they have the Department of Security number down at the station?"

"No, no, sir! The day before yesterday, when I was standing by your desk, while you were writing, I noticed the number of your telephone on the desk."

"All right, then, hit the road. And remember: 24 hours!"

Then I heard hollowly, "Captain, set up surveillance on Borodin again, now!" And he hung up.

"Did you record all of it?" I asked my stenographer agent.

"Yes, sir, all of it."

"Did you hear all of this?" I asked the yard keeper.

"I sure did, all of it. But frankly, mister chief, I think this whole thing will end up in murder!" the yard keeper responded very seriously.

"Well, think all you want!" I replied, laughing.

Borodin, who had witnessed the whole scene, was numb with fear.

Apparently, he was struggling with contradictory feelings. On the one hand, the fear before the formidable Chief of the Department of Security was still living within him. On the other hand, he saw that I had no doubt that there was a fraud taking place. Yet, he must have been thinking, "What if the Chief of Police is mistaken?" I could read this complicated range of feelings on his worried, flushed face.

By four o'clock, I sent my assistant V. E. Andreev with four agents to Skatertny Lane to arrest the people in the "Department of Security." I recommended him to invite the district police officer and a detail of police to come with him, but V. E. Andreev apparently found it unnecessary and went to accomplish the mission alone, thinking he could carry it out on his own.

In an hour, he called me and reported:

"Arkady Frantsevich, there's an unexpected complication here. We arrested three men dressed like gendarmes and a woman who was in the apartment, but we sort of missed Gilevich. He slipped to the back room, locked himself in, and barricaded the door. He says that at the slightest attempt from our side to break into his shelter, he will shoot us down like dogs with a revolver that he says he has with him. What do we do now?"

There was nothing I could do but go down there myself. I knew that the brothers Gilevich were rather "inventive" and played hard, so I picked up a bulletproof vest from the police station and put it on. I took a briefcase with a plate put into it made of the same material that comprised the vest. When I arrived to Skatertny Lane, I shielded my head with the briefcase and came up to the door which hid Gilevich.

"Hey, you, over there, Port Arthur hero under siege[18], surrender! Don't make us break down the door!"

Gilevich recognized my voice right away and angrily responded:

"So, you came to get the third brother, now?"

"I don't really remember how many brothers we've already got. But I see that each of you is remarkable in his own way!"

"What do you want from me?"

"First, come out, Mister Chief of the Department of Security, and then we'll talk."

"I wouldn't recommend you, Mr. Koshko, to approach the door, otherwise you'll catch a bullet in your head!"

"Stop acting like a fool, Gilevich. Do not make me resort to the extreme measures. You know how armed resistance to the authorities can come back to haunt you."

There was a long pause. Then the lock clicked, the door quickly swung open (the barricades apparently existed in Andreev's imagination only), and Vasily Gilevich appeared in the doorway.

"I surrender!" was the first thing he said. "You are lucky I didn't have Andrei's drops with me (he meant the potassium cyanide that his brother, Prilutsky's killer, used to poison himself), otherwise you'd never get me alive!"

He was immediately handcuffed and taken to the police station.

The search in the apartment resulted in positively nothing.

"So, Gilevich, let's talk now," I said to him in my office. "First of all, where is the 5,000 rubles that you took away from Borodin?"

---

[18] A reference to the Siege of Port Arthur, the longest and most violent battle of the Russo-Japanese War (1904-1905).

133

"What 5,000?"

"Aha! Are you saying you don't know what I am talking about? Maybe you'll also say that you don't know Borodin and that he didn't come to you the day before yesterday?"

"I do know Borodin, and he indeed came to me the day before yesterday. We discussed an order of bricks, but this is the first I have heard anything about 5,000 rubles."

"Well, now that's stupid. You must understand that in your situation the only thing that can mitigate your punishment is frank confession, and instead you're talking rubbish. I do have live witnesses against you."

"Listen, Mr. Koshko. I see you think I am a total fool, and you're naïvely trying to trick me! I repeat that this is the first time I have heard about the money. Besides, I only talked to Borodin in private, without any witnesses."

"Is that what you think?"

"It's not only that I think so, but also that you cannot prove otherwise."

I pressed the bell button.

"Please invite the witnesses!" I ordered.

The stenographer and the yard keeper entered the office.

"Would you be so kind," I addressed to the stenographer, "to read what you heard and recorded."

The agent read aloud the record of my phone conversation with Gilevich. He reproduced it with absolute precision. I addressed to both witnesses.

"Would you testify under oath that you heard this conversation with your own ears?"

"We would, right away, sir!"

Gilevich was sitting there, gaping and goggling his eyes, for quite a while. Finally, he pronounced:

"Well! Now I guess there's nothing left for me to do but tell the truth. But, for God's sake, satisfy my curiosity. Explain this amazing mystery to me!"

"I will. But first you have to provide your frank testimony."

Gilevich confessed to everything and told about his imposture and dressing his friends as gendarmes. The apartment was provided to him by another friend, a technician, who had left for vacation for twenty-eight days and had no idea about the criminal events going on there. Gilevich also told me that if he had received the other 5,000 rubles from Borodin, he would have disappeared from Moscow without trace at once—he intended to go abroad the next day, where, according to him, he had been preparing an affair of a global scale.

"How about your mystery?" he asked me.

"Here it is!" I pointed at the telephone and two branch receivers. Gilevich slapped himself on the forehead and burst into bitter laughter.

The court sentenced him to one and a half years of penal battalions and attainder. The jury was merciful toward his accomplices: They were acquitted.

The Theft at Count Mellin's

A grand larceny was committed in the Kreis Wenden province of the Governorate of Livonia, on the estate of Count Mellin.

As far as I remember, it happened in the early 90s. Investigating a larceny in this county was not under my jurisdiction, but the count complained to the local governor, M. A. Pashkov, about the inaction of Wenden's police, so the governor proposed that I take over the case.

According to the governor, a certain amount of valuables had been stolen from the count: over one-hundred pounds of silver, several items of gold flatware, a whole box of small diamonds, a collection of old miniatures, several precious ornaments belonging to the countess, interest bearing securities, and so on.

I took two functionaries with me, Grundman and Lein, and took off.

Count Mellin's estate was magnificent. The descendant of Livonian knights who had settled down here several centuries ago, Count Mellin had surrounded himself with the most pompous luxury. His house was a real palace.

I and my companions were given a whole luxury suite. We arrived early in the morning and were received by a steward or majordomo.

We were immediately served an elegantly arranged tea, and the steward informed me that the count had appointed an audience with me for twelve o'clock.

Indeed, I was received at noon exactly. The count spoke politely, but majestically. He asked me to apply all my efforts to solving this crime, and then he announced that the countess's "appearance" was to be right before breakfast.

It really was an "appearance." She came up to the table wearing fine attire, in diamonds, surrounded by several dependents who apparently acted as maids of honor in her retinue.

As the countess was speaking about the theft, she expressed especial pity concerning the loss of a small gold book in which she would write down the names of men to whom she had promised a dance. On the lid of this small book, according to her, was an amazing miniature, and underneath it was a tiny little clock, the size of a silver ten-kopeck coin or even smaller—a real masterpiece!

The local police chief was invited to the breakfast, too. As I talked to him after the breakfast, I concluded that the investigation had been being handled extremely negligently and superficially.

The first thing I did was examine the scene. The items had been stolen from a safe of the most innovative structure. It was situated in a small room next to the count's study. The room was on the first floor, beside only ceremonial halls and servants' rooms. There were two doors leading outside: the main entrance and a door to the garden through a glass terrace. The garden abutted a lake that was about 3,500 feet wide; one could see the woods on the other side of the lake. The safe's keys were kept in a drawer of the count's desk, which was known only to the steward who received us.

The house was always in perfect, German order. The count himself checked all the locks before going to sleep, so getting inside the house at night without breaking the locks or having some assistance from inside was unthinkable. There had been three days between the moment when the count checked his safe for the last time and the moment when the theft was discovered. During this time, the thieves could have been doing whatever they wanted with the stolen things. We should add another week to that for the time spent by the local police chief on his fruitless searches. Such a long period of time, of course, not only allowed the thieves to thoroughly hide what they had stolen, but also to cover their tracks.

Thorough examination of the safe's and doors' locks showed that they all were opened with keys, because lock picks, even if used most carefully, leave scratches.

I asked the count if he trusted his steward.

"As I trust myself!" he replied. "Meyer has been living in my house for twenty years, and he is devoted to me, spiritually and physically. Besides, I have put him under exceptionally favorable circumstances: I have built a home for him, I gave him 135 acres of land, and his sons obtained higher education degrees with my support. Whatever people say, thankfulness is not an empty word, and it surely can't be alien to my Meyer. Concerning the rest of the employees, please ask him in reference to them. I am not usually interested in them, letting Meyer himself hire the staff of servants."

When I finished the search and received the count's reference to his steward, I found myself in a deadlock. The weight of the stolen things was almost 350 pounds. In order to take so much away from the house and get away with it all, one would need several accomplices and, I guessed, horses as well.

In the evening, Grundman and Lein came back after spending the whole day in the surroundings.

They didn't find any rumors that would help the investigation. People spoke well of the countess. The count was described as a very stingy man who would weigh his employees' bread precisely to the gram.

"Can you provide me with an exact list of all servants, those who work here or were working within past year?" I asked Meyer.

"Oh, yes, of course! I am a careful man, so I have a special book for this. If you would like, I will even make notes in the margin indicating which employee was fired for what and when."

"Great! Please do so."

I addressed the local chief of police with the same request.

Shortly the steward gave me the lists with about forty names overall in in. Written next to some of them were: "fired for stealing desserts," "inclined to rudeness," "devoid of neatness," etc.

We looked through the list, but didn't find a single name familiar to us from the criminal world of Riga.

"Tell me, please," I asked the steward, "were the woods on the other side of the lake searched?"

"Yes, the local chief has searched it."

However, I decided to conduct this search again, and thoroughly—on the next day.

I invited the local police chief and asked him:

"Did you search the woods well?"

"We didn't search the woods at all."

"What do you mean, you didn't? Why does Meyer say you did?"

"I don't know."

I summoned the steward and registered my surprise to him. He acted oddly, hummed and hawed, and started saying how I misunderstood him, because indeed the woods weren't searched, etc.

"Fine. I don't need you for now. I want to talk to the police chief."

The steward reluctantly left, and it seemed to me that he hadn't walked away from the door after he closed it. I quickly swung it open and almost hit Meyer. He started greasily offering me tea, pretending that he had come back exactly for that.

"Thank you! We don't want any tea. Leave us alone, please."

Meyer bowed and left—actually left this time.

"By the way, you've asked me for a list of employees," the police chief said to me, "so here you go. I took it from the Grange Police."

I didn't even know such an institution existed.

I compared this list to the steward's list and, to my surprise, found the name of a certain Otto Villnes in it, the count's former footman who had been fired a year before. He wasn't mentioned in the steward's list.

I shared my discovery with my agents, and Grundman said to me:

"Otto Villnes? I know this name very well. You weren't yet working in Riga, sir, back when we prosecuted him for a grand larceny. I even remember his nickname among thieves—'vize-fräulein,' which means 'old maid.'"

It looked like we found the thieves' trail.

I ordered my agents to keep this information secret for some time, because not only did we have to find the thieves, but also find the stolen things. Likewise, we could not inform Meyer of our assumptions, since he was obviously involved in the larceny and could warn his accomplices about danger.

I paid special attention to the woods because it looked like the stolen things were most likely transported through them. Carrying the stolen things from the house to the lake was not that difficult—in order to do that, one had to walk approximately 200 feet through the garden. Boats were right there. One could load the stolen things on one of them, go to the opposite shore, and then easily put them into a cart that the thieves had hidden somewhere in the thickets. There was the beginning of the road there that went through the woods and led to neighboring villages.

The next morning about thirty people, headed by me, Grundman and Lein, went to the woods. They occupied a rather significant area of approximately one-thousand acres.

The large area is why, to start with, I decided to first search the road and the lane next to it, about 1,500 feet wide. After several hours or searching, we found empty oak boxes, in which silver used to be stored, under a nut shrub. Even more, Grundman recognized the place and said that at the end of the road was a mill that belonged to Otto Villnes's brother. In the evening, we returned to the house. When the count saw the boxes we had found, he seemed to be inspired with a little hope.

Further searches in the woods resulted in nothing.

I thought that staying any longer at the count's estate was unnecessary, so we returned to Riga. But before the departure, I went to the nearest post office to see the postmaster.

"Are you familiar with steward Meyer's handwriting?"

"Of course, I am."

"Would you please be so kind to open and inspect all the letters he sends and all the letters he receives? Of course, I would ask you to keep this in complete secrecy."

Upon my arrival in Riga, I immediately began searching for Otto Villnes.

According to the information bureau, he was not in the city. I decided to send an agent to the mill owned by Villnes's brother. This errand would be rather difficult, since the agent would have to look through the mill and get to know people who live there without provoking any suspicions, while the Villneses were extremely distrustful and cautious—they knew the possible ruses of investigation thanks to their past.

That is why we came up with the following plan.

There was an evangelic society in Riga that distributed printed versions of the Gospels among the people of the governorate. Among its members were a lot of agents walking around the governorate with special bags filled with holy books. I went to this society and managed to get credentials, a bag and ten copies of the Gospels for my agent Lein so that he could go to the mill. He walked from the train station to the mill, all on foot, bare-headed, deeply pensive while reading the Holy Scriptures. At the mill, he met Villnes's brother, but "vize-fräulein" was absent. In fact, Lein came back with nothing. The only thing he did learn was that the Villneses were Meyer's nephews on their mother's side.

I started creating a new plan to find the thieves, when suddenly I received a copy of a letter made by the postmaster. This was the steward's letter to Otto Villnes. It was addressed to Riga, and the text was:

"Dear Otto:

Recently, a hunting company came to our land from Riga. They hunted in the woods, killed something, but then lost any trail of game and went back.

It is quiet and peaceful over here again."

I immediately dashed to the address on the letter with my agents. The apartment we found was not registered to Villnes, but we found his mother in it.

"Where is your son?" I asked her.

"Otto went to Petersburg the day before yesterday."

"Where is he staying in Petersburg?"

"I don't know that; he hasn't written to me yet."

We searched the apartment, but we didn't find any of the items stolen from the count. But Grundman noticed that the old lady was holding a book in her hands all the time, without letting it go for a second. He took the book from her, went through its pages, and found a sealed letter addressed to steward Meyer. We opened the envelope. The content of the letter was as follows:

"Dear uncle:

I am heading to the station now, going to Petersburg. I wanted to reply to today's letter as soon as possible. I am glad the hunting company has left you. All's quiet here as well. But I have to communicate sad news to you, about the death of poor Janis, who died on Saturday and was buried five days ago. I went to the cemetery and brought our tears to his grave.

Wait for further news from me,

Yours,

Otto"

"Who is this deceased Janis your son is talking about?" I asked Villnes's mother.

"I don't know. There's so many people he knows!"

142

"Why do you have this letter?"

"When my son was leaving, he asked me to send it, but I never made it."

I left one agent in Villnes's apartment and started the attempts to identify deceased Janis. It was important for us to find his grave because, as Grundman explained to me, the word for 'tears' in Lettish was widely used instead of the word 'diamonds.' That is why we had grounds to assume that in his letter Otto was talking about diamonds buried in Janis's grave.

All the Orthodox, Lutheran, Catholic churches and synagogues of Riga were asked for information on a person named Janis, whose funeral was performed within the previous week. We received negative responses from every place. I was completely confused, but a priest of one parish church advised me to ask the priests of two regiments accommodated in Riga: Izborsky Regiment and Maloyaroslavsky Regiment.

It turned out that the previous week there was a requiem for a soldier of the 4th company, Ivan Libus, in the house church of the Maloyaroslavsky Regiment. He was buried at the regimental cemetery. His dormitory companions always called him Janis.

Having this information, I went to the archbishop of Riga, told him about the case, and asked for permission to open and search Janis's grave. His Eminence gave me a very diplomatic response.

"I cannot give my permission to open the grave of a deceased Christian, for it is against the canons of our church. But it is not prohibited to anyone, however, to put a grave in order, to bring it to a more splendid appearance. You could edge it with turf, extract and renew the cross, enlarge the grave mound. If you wish to perform such kinds of restoration, I will not raise difficulties on your way."

Of course, I expressed my ardent willingness to beautify Janis's grave, and thus received blessing and written permission from His Eminence. Then I went to the military cemetery with two agents.

I took a policeman and the cemetery's watchman with me as witnesses. We easily found Janis's grave and set to searching through it. We took out the cross and dug through the grave mound, where we found a big steel needle case, at the depth of about four feet. The needle case was filled with diamonds.

We drew up a report, and then put the grave in order and put the cross back.

After two weeks "vize-fräulein" still wasn't back from Petersburg. I sent Lein to the mill again, this time ordering him to approach Villnes's property from the opposite end of the road and with an empty bag, as if he was coming back after a successful round. But Otto wasn't at the mill, just like the first time.

However, shortly the postmaster forwarded another of Villnes's letters to me. It was again addressed to his uncle. We learned from it that Otto had moved from Petersburg to Reval[19] and was hired as a footman by Baron M. He informed his uncle that soon there would be a "job" to do.

We rushed to Reval, easily found Baron M., and finally arrested 'vize-fräulein.' This nickname amazingly suited him: He was a tall, dry man with completely hairless face, sensitive, sentimental and whining, with a squeaky woman's voice. He really looked like an old maid.

At his interrogation, "vize-fräulein" resolutely denied his guilt.

Since his arrest couldn't be a secret to his accomplices, I immediately went to the mill for the search. Otto's brother was struck as by thunder when I showed up with Inspector Lein, who had recently visited his house disguised as a humble book peddler. When we arrived at the mill, Villnes must have smelled a rat, as he grabbed a piece of paper and shoved it in his mouth. However, it was immediately extracted and turned out to be the steward's note in which Meyer informed his nephew that he had heard from Otto from Reval.

We arrested the brother, although a thorough search through the entire building of the mill resulted in nothing.

---

[19] Reval is the former name of Tallinn

Upon my return to Riga, I was informed that Otto Villnes attempted suicide by scratching the vein on his wrist with a small piece of iron that he had taken off the lace of his own boot. He was saved from death only because a prison guard randomly had checked on him. Otto was sent to the prison hospital, where the doctor promised his swift recovery.

In a few days, the chief of the prison hospital called me on the telephone and informed me that Villnes's mother had come to her unwell son, and when she was leaving the hospital, she had a Holy Bible in her hands that Otto had given her. The book was taken away from her. It was an ordinary copy of the Holy Bible, of a small size. I started to attentively leaf through it, looking for signs, underlined letters, etc.

I didn't find any conventional code. I separated the book's back and noticed a clear, white, small piece of paper glued to it. I carefully unstuck it, turned it over, and saw tiny lines of writing. With a magnifying glass, I managed to read the following: "Janis Libus, the 4th company of Maloyaroslavsky Regiment, died November 5, buried at the regimental cemetery. I brought our tears to his grave." Below was a drawing of the grave cross, and a pencil mark was underneath it.

Apparently, Otto's mother managed to let him know that his letter addressed to his uncle was taken away from her by us, so Villnes decided to inform the steward again of the place where the diamonds were.

Neither of them knew that I had photographed this letter and sent the original copy to the intended addressee.

The case was already quite solved, so I decided it was time to arrest Meyer. Agents who I sent to Count Mellin's estate later told me that the count was extremely outraged and by all means resisted the arrest of his steward, calling it an inconsistent, cruel, and unnecessary action. But my order was flat, so in spite of the count's protest, Meyer was arrested and brought to Riga.

In a few days, as soon as Otto Villnes recovered, I summoned him to my office.

"Here's the deal, Villnes," I said. "It is the last time I am calling you for interrogation. If you want, you can confess; if you don't, don't confess. It's up to you. The evidence against you is absolutely incontrovertible. Your Uncle Meyer and your brother are arrested, and they have already confessed to everything and told us (here I took a shot, of course) how you transported the stolen things on a boat at night."

"Vize-fräulein" distrustfully smiled.

"Do not think I'm just saying this in order to catch you out. I repeat. They have confessed to everything, and here's the proof: They gave up the diamonds that you had buried at the regimental cemetery under Janis's cross. Here they are! (I took the needle box out of my pocket and poured the diamonds on my desk.) Here's Meyer's note to your brother, which is also evidence against you all. Here's your letter from Reval addressed to your uncle. Here's the piece of paper that was stuck to the back of a Bible. Finally, it wasn't your clear conscience that made you attempt suicide, was it? Is that enough? Remember that frank confession will mitigate your punishment."

"Vize-fräulein," struck by the evidence, upset about the loss of the diamonds, believing that his uncle and brother had confessed to everything, found further denial unbeneficial and completely acknowledged his guilt.

With the expansiveness inherent in him, he started to flagellate himself, not only showering himself with contemptuous epithets and cursing, but also convulsively tearing out tufts of his already sparse hair.

"Let's go, let's go, mister chief! I'll show you where the things are buried. What belongs to the count, give back to him. Do not spare us swindlers! We get what we deserve; we belong where we're going."

I didn't want to let the moment slip away or give "vize-fräulein" time to change his mind, so I immediately made arrangements via the telephone for a steam locomotive and a heated van, took four agents with me and left with Otto Villnes for the Hincenberg station that he indicated. In the woods, not far from the station, he led us to a shrub and said, "It's here."

Using crowbars and shovels, we broke and threw about somewhat frozen ground and dug out a big, tall Landrin fruit-drops box. Inside it were rolled-up interest-bearing securities and two bracelets with empty sockets where stones had been.

"Vize-fräulein" had sold the stones upon his arrival to Petersburg.

Next to the tin box was a match box with the countess's small notebook in it, the one with a miniature and a clock. Unfortunately, an accidental blow of a shovel chopped a piece of the miniature off and crushed the clock.

"Vize-fräulein" led us on from this shrub, guided by the broken twigs on the trees, to the next cache.

There turned out to be ten caches overall.

All the stolen things were found, but, unfortunately, not everything had been preserved. Huge silver dishes, for example, were chopped into pieces—obviously in order to make it easier to hide them.

My assumptions on how the theft was performed proved fully right. According to the confession of the accused, everything was carried out the following way: The brothers Villnes sneaked into the garden at night, came up to the glass terrace and were given the precious load by their uncle, steward Meyer, who had taken the count's keys from his desk drawer, opened the safe, and taken all the valuables out of it. In several trips, the brothers transferred the stolen things from the terrace to the lake, loaded it on a boat, then went to the opposite shore, and put all the things on a cart that had been prepared for that. One of them pushed the cart, and the other one went back to give the key to the boat chain back to their uncle.

The count revealed a rather peculiar psychology toward Meyer. He took up his former steward's case trying to mitigate his fate.

Meyer, in his turn, expressed no contrition and referred to the count with hatred and irritation.

After all of this, how can one restrain oneself from saying that thankfulness is an empty word?

Stake a Million on Monk

I give this somewhat odd title to this short story only because one cunning and quite eccentric fraud was filed under this label by the Moscow police back in the day, and this is the fraud I am going to tell you about.

A certain man named Strelbitsky, a big soap manufacturer, once came to see me and said:

"Sir, I have come to you to consult concerning an affair that I became incredibly interested in. An extremely profitable offer was made to me, but it is so strange that I don't even know what to think about it. In fact, please take a look at it yourself." He handed me a letter.

The letter read:

"Dear Sir:

After making diverse inquiries regarding you, we managed to learn with indubitable precision not only about the general picture of your trading affairs, but also about your morals. You appear to be a good, honest man, and your soap enterprise appears to be a reputable and promising business. We also learned that you are currently seeking money to expand your business. All of these factors combined to impel us to address ourselves to you with the following, completely secret offer.

We can loan you one million rubles under conditions that are extremely profitable to you and quite substantial to us.

The matter is that a certain archimandrite (who is also the father superior) living in one of the remote monasteries in the

148

province possesses an account in one of the banks, containing one million rubles deposited as a four-percent government annuity payable to the bearer. A few years ago, the indicated archimandrite gave in to sin and came together with a certain woman, an amazingly beautiful woman, to be blunt, and begat a child, a boy who is now six years old.

You know, of course, that along with taking monastic vows and rejecting the world, monks lose their civil rights as well: family rights, rights of inheritance, etc. Thus the archimandrite, as he is ill and feels his death approaching, is very much preoccupied with thoughts about his son. He cannot bequeath the deposit to him and does not wish, because of certain reasons, to transfer it to the mother. That is why he entrusted me to find a reliable, honest, and wealthy man who would take care of this young life, the life that is so dear to his father, and would preserve the money until the boy attains his majority. As a reward for this favor, the archimandrite offers exceptionally profitable conditions of the loan.

You are offered one million rubles under a bill for a term of fifteen years with annual payments of only one percent, or 10,000 rubles, which you oblige yourself to pass to the mother for her living and raising the child. Your good conscience, of course, is given an opportunity to make more of this money by the day of the child's majority, but this is not your obligation.

All that is required of you is to release regular annual payments to the mother and retire the bill in fifteen years. If you find the described offer acceptable, please respond immediately to Smolensk, post office, to be called for by the receipt No. 1462."

As soon as I raised my eyes after reading this curious message, Strelbitsky hastily asked me:

"So, what do you think of all this?"

"I think someone is trying to swindle you."

"Is that so?"

"Of course! It's not only that the offer itself is too fantastic, but also I seem to remember hearing some vague rumors about similar tricks in the province. One should think the "operators" have transferred their work to the capitals, now trying to catch some unsuspecting souls here."

My visitor embarrassedly smiled and said in a cheerless voice:

"You know, I thought the offer was so tempting that I actually have already sent my response to Smolensk stating that I consented in principle."

"Ah, is that so? And?"

"Nothing so far. I am waiting for the reply."

"Then why have you come to me?"

"You see, I wrote in the heat of the moment, and then I gave it some thought and I had doubts. Now after what you've said, my doubts have turned into certainty, so I will refuse this peculiar affair."

"That is the right thing. However, I would like to ask you, for the common good, to help me solve this mystery and find the enterprising swindlers."

"At your service. But how can I help you?"

"Would you bring me the response you will receive from Smolensk?"

"Yes. I promise I will."

Thus we parted.

In three days Strelbitsky came to me with the response.

"D.S.:

Following the willingness you have expressed, we hereby appoint the day, hour and place of our future meeting. We request that you arrive in Smolensk, come to Lopatinsky Garden on July 7 at ten o'clock in the morning, and take a seat on the fifth bench to the right on the main walkway, counting from the restaurant. I will meet you and show you a bank certificate of deposit for you to examine.

The whole procedure will not take more than two days, so you do not have to bring additional money with you. Concerning the bill forms, they, of course, can be purchased here, so there is no need for you to worry about them and bring them all the way from Moscow.

The archimandrite thanks God for finally finding a man whose good name will guarantee the success of this matter that is so dear to his heart.

Looking forward to our near and pleasant meeting."

After reading this response, I became pensive. I had solved many different frauds and all kinds of fanciful swindles within previous years, but each of them demonstrated its inner soul, the sense, if I may say, of the attempted fraud. And here I couldn't figure out the interest of the criminal scheme. Why would criminals summon a person to Smolensk and appoint a meeting with him in daylight in a public place? Obviously, it was not about violence or robbery. Why would they invent the complicated procedure with a fifteen-year bill without even proposing at least to buy at a bargain an artfully counterfeited certificate of deposit? Because a person wouldn't sign a million rubles-worth bill without thoroughly examining the bank document or making inquiries in the bank concerning the deposit, would he? Then what would the frauds count on, dealing with an experienced and serious businessman? I was searching my mind in vain without finding an answer. This case got me interested to such extent that not only did I decide to send experienced agents to Smolensk, but also to go there myself.

My appearance and build were dramatically different from Strelbitsky's, which is why I thought it was necessary to give this part to my talented agent Schwabo instead of saving it for myself. Even without any makeup, Schwabo somewhat resembled Strelbitsky. This precaution could have been unnecessary because Strelbitsky had never met any of the frauds in person. He only communicated with them through letters. However, I thought it was possible that the frauds could have caught a glimpse of him at some point when exploring the lifestyle of their victim-to-be. So, by July 7, Schwabo departed for Smolensk, having a passport for the name Strelbitsky and trying to get the feel for his role as the latter. I was on the same train with two agents. In Smolensk, Schwabo was staying in one hotel, while we were in another one.

At ten o'clock in the morning, Schwabo was already sitting in Lopatinsky Garden on the indicated bench with a wallet tightly filled with "doublets" (which is tautly pressed newsprint wrapped with one-hundred-ruble bills) and a pile of inexpensive bill forms. Meanwhile, my people and I were casually walking not far from him. Soon, a decently dressed man appeared, came up to Schwabo, and sat down on the bench. I saw them bow to each other shortly and shake hands, and then a lively conversation began between them. The unknown character took some paper. Schwabo carefully looked at it and then pulled out his wallet that looked like an unfolded accordion. Then they said goodbye to each other, shaking each other's hands for a long while, and Schwabo went to his hotel.

Shortly he reported to me:

"Everything went smoothly. I guess my filled wallet made an impression. However, when I told him I had bought bill forms in Moscow, he for some reason said reproachfully, without hiding his vexation, 'Why would you do this? I wrote to you that those can easily be found here, in Smolensk!' He appointed the next meeting tomorrow, at one, at the same bench, and promised to introduce me to the child's mother as she is, of course, interested in meeting with, if I can put it this way, the future caregiver of her son. The certificate of deposit that he showed to me didn't seem to provoke any suspicions judging by the way it looked. It was a regular bank sheet made of thick parchment paper, all the stamps and signatures of directors and the teller were there—in short, it was just the way it should be.

Tomorrow I am supposed to meet the mother, and after that, we decided to go straight to the garden's restaurant and have breakfast in a private room, where I will have a chance to scrutinize the certificate of deposit in detail once again. We decided that then we would go to the state bank office, where I will make sure the deposit indicated in the document is in place. Then I will have to fill in my bill forms and immediately exchange them in the presence of a notary and witnesses for a certificate of deposit. Along with the bills, I will sign and hand over the agreement written in the restaurant about paying ten-thousand rubles to the child's mother annually."

"Where's the trick here, Schwabo? What do you think?"

"I have no idea, sir! At first I thought that the sticking point was that the victim must have at least 8,000 rubles in his pocket when coming to the garden, which is the amount necessary for purchasing a million-ruble bill. But then why would they appoint a meeting in such a crowded place? That's first, and second—I told them that bill forms were already prepared and purchased by me in Moscow, therefore I might as well not have a lot of money on me. On the other hand, the fraud saw my wallet tightly filled with money, and maybe that is why he keeps playing this game. I have to say there's absolute chaos in my head, and I also have to confess that sometimes it seems to me that the whole story wasn't made up, but is actually true, the way those people describe it."

"Come on, Schwabo, you're out of your mind! Wait until tomorrow, and I guess everything will be clarified in the restaurant's room."

The next day we established the following plan: As soon as they were about to rewrite the agreement about the mother's annual pension with ink (its draft being written with a pencil), two of my agents and I would storm into the room and arrest the man and the woman. The signal for me would be the footman's coming out of the room to get the ink.

The next day Schwabo entered Lopatinsky Garden from one side, while I and two my agents entered it from the other side, at one, precisely. Schwabo sat down on his bench, and I watched from a distance. Shortly, the character from yesterday showed up, arm in arm with an amazingly beautiful woman.

He greeted Schwabo in a friendly manner, and the latter jumped up to gallantly kiss the hand that the woman had majestically held out to him. After spending some time on the bench, they got up and went to the summer restaurant. They mounted the porch, turned to the corridor, and disappeared into one of the private rooms. My people and I occupied a table on the porch. Our position was convenient because all the private rooms opened on the corridor, and everything that was to be carried to the rooms was inevitably carried past us. We had to wait for a long time, about two hours. Finally, a footman appeared, asked for an inkpot and a pen at the counter, and disappeared again behind the room's door. I winked to my people, and we followed the footman.

When we stormed into the room, Schwabo's interlocutor got to the open window in the twinkling of an eye—my agent caught him by the feet at the very last moment. The woman quickly crumpled the document and shoved it into her mouth and started convulsively chewing. We didn't let her finish her "tasty breakfast" and extracted the paper from her mouth. It turned out to be the same certificate of deposit.

We took the arrested to the local police department, where at the entrance an unexpected scene unfolded. A gentleman was coming out of the department, saw the man we had arrested, and screamed blue murder. "That's him! That is yesterday's scoundrel, the fraud who robbed me! Ah, that bastard! Bring him, gentlemen. Bring him right to the chief!"

It turned out that the man yelling had fallen victim to our swindler on the previous day. He was tempted by the same monk's imaginary million, so he had come from Kiev to Smolensk, purchased bill papers for a particular amount of money from the local treasurer's office, following the trickster's instructions, and invited both cheats to his hotel room as he didn't want to go to a restaurant. During the breakfast, they put some powder into his wine so that he fell asleep, and when he woke up, he saw that the bill forms were gone, along with 1,800 rubles.

The mystery was finally solved. Conspiring with the frauds was one of the tellers of the local governorate treasurer's office. The cheats would send their unsuspecting victims to him to purchase bill papers. Upon completion of the crime, the treasurer accepted unfilled bill forms back at a discount of 10 percent. This discount was his profit in this scheme.

In cases when the victims already had blanks with them, these blanks would be either accepted by the same teller, or the frauds would send them to Warsaw, at some discount as well.

Thus, at every turn, the tricksters gained at least 8,000 rubles—usually even more, because aside from bill paper their victims often had some additional money on them just in case.

According to their confession, Schwabo would be their seventh victim. After rewriting the agreement with ink, they were going to order a bottle of champagne to celebrate a good start and put some narcotic powder into Schwabo's glass.

This is how this witty fraud was solved, revealing the thoughtless credulity of six sedate Russian businessmen who were fooled by the stories of an archimandrite's legendary million.

300,000 Rubles on a Counterfeit Appropriation Ticket

A certain person came to Moscow's Governorate Treasury, showed an appropriation ticket[20] signed by one of Moscow's magistrates, and received 300,000 rubles deposited under the magistrate's name.

In about two weeks, the deposit owner requested information about the deposit's status, and it was revealed that 300,000 rubles had been released based on an appropriation ticket. A whole fuss started because the deposit owner had never signed such a ticket. As a result, we were notified by the Governorate Treasury about the forgery, and I got to work.

A thorough examination of the ticket showed that the three last figures of the six-figure number had been carefully and quite artfully rubbed off and replaced.

It should be mentioned that appropriation tickets for different kinds of expenses used to be given in series of one hundred or more to each institution. Thus, by using the number of a ticket, one always could find out who the public officer was and whose office issued that ticket. The number on the counterfeit ticket led us to one of Moscow magistrates. But just as we expected, we found nothing: His documents were fine, and the appropriation ticket under that number hadn't even been used.

---

[20] Appropriation ticket is a document that permits allocating a particular amount of money from the public budget to the bearer

Thus there was a need to find by any means what the figures were that had been rubbed off and replaced on the counterfeit document. The task wasn't easy. But the police's talented photographer von Mengden eagerly set to work and finally achieved the goal after a week or so of hard work. By merging photographs and taking pictures of those complicated combinations of previously constructed images, he managed to make residual, unseen, elusive silhouettes of rubbed-off figures brighter and more detectable, and finally after an infinite number of such manipulations and magnifications, he got to the point where those figures were visible to a naked eye. We thus revealed the true initial number of the ticket.

The number belonged to the series of tickets of one of the magistrates of Zamoskvorechye, a certain R., whose brother was a well-known member of the State Duma[21] and later almost became the Minister of Finland Affairs during the time of Kerensky[22]. I decided to visit him.

He received me according to the code of liberal morals.

He tried to express offence, contempt, and disgust on his generally lackluster face. My arguments about the necessity to examine his records due to the revealed forgery, in which he might have been unintentionally involved, didn't convince this clever man. He pompously stated that he wouldn't allow the police (to be specific: "this contemptible institution") to rummage through his items and documents. Not only was I disgusted to insist, but even to talk to this narcissistic liberal idiot, so I addressed myself to the Prosecutor of the Judicial Court, Mr. Khrulev. The latter referred to the magistrate with a rather uncomplimentary epithet, which nevertheless wasn't about his intelligence, apologized to me on the behalf of the judiciary, assigned a judicial investigator to me, and gave us permission to examine the records of Mr. R.

Before I went to the magistrate for the second time, I made an inquiry to the Governorate Treasury, and the response was that the indicated appropriation ticket (we provided them with the real number

---

[21] The State Duma is the lower house of the Parliament of Russia

[22] Alexander Kerensky was the Minister-Chairman of the Russian Provisional Government in July–November 1917

156

that was defined by our photographer) was not used to release any funds.

I immediately requested information about all the office employees of Mr. R. It turned out that all office affairs were run by a certain clerk named Andrei Boitsov. It so happened that my agent Leontiev, who was a specialist in surveillance over staffs of employees of both public and private institutions, was acquainted with Boitsov. According to Leontiev, Boitsov was a great scum, a bribe taker who would wring profit out of his job by all means, like counseling the accused or illegally hindering the execution of the orders.

I wanted to use this fortunate acquaintance and ordered Leontiev to meet Boitsov somewhere and talk to him. The latter, of course, had no idea Leontiev worked for the police.

"Order a couple of glasses of wine, Leontiev," I said to him, "and try to get some information. Maybe Boitsov will blab something."

The next day Leontiev "accidentally" ran into Boitsov in a tavern and started a conversation. He told him that he had been broke for a while, without a job, but now he had found one as an office manager at a district chair's office. Boitsov was lively and talked a lot, but he didn't even mention "the affair." I kept the surveillance over Boitsov on for three days, but it resulted in positively nothing. Obviously, Boitsov had been disturbed by my visit to his boss, so he was extremely careful and didn't go anywhere except for his apartment, his work, and a tavern.

I came up with a plan of further action. I was sure that if I had visited R. again, I would find something wrong in his office records, since a ticket for a counterfeit document was taken from R.'s series. But Boitsov would of course get away with it, so what should I do next?

Then I got an idea: I needed to use the acquaintance of Boitsov and Leontiev, or their meeting to be more precise, one more time.

I ordered my agents who were watching Boitsov to avoid being careful and to let the clerk notice the surveillance. They carried it out precisely according to my order.

Equipped with this information, I came to R. with the judicial investigator. He received us as dryly as before, but this time he couldn't resist the inspection of his records. I examined the ticket book in his office, and among the counterfoils of used tickets, I found one that had the number we needed on it (the real, initial number that we had photographically restored on the counterfeit ticket). But the counterfoil read a different name, subject, and the amount was not 300,000 rubles, but 10,000.

It was obvious that the counterfoil was filled with made-up text for the sake of deceit, while the actual ticket was used for the fraudulent counterfeiting aimed at gaining 300,000 rubles.

When we informed Mr. R. about the result of the inspection of his records, we drove him to great confusion and perplexity. Where did his arrogant tone go? He suddenly became cloyingly courteous, brought me a chair himself, and started persuading me sweetly to sit down. Apparently, the "liberal principles" gave place to fear and self-interest.

"I will have to arrest Boitsov," I said to him.

"How can that be, Mr. Koshko? Do you really suspect this honest, bright fellow? He has been working for me for more than a year now, and I can't stop praising him."

"You may praise him as much as you want, but I happen to know for sure that this 'honest' Boitsov person is nothing but a swindler who often arranges his affairs by using your name as a cover. After all, it's Boitsov's handwriting that we found on the counterfoil of your book."

"Well, you are the doctor, Mr. Koshko. Do what you think you should do! Please, feel free!" said Mr. R. with a charming smile.

I went back to the office and came up to Boitsov.

He was a character of around 35, with an extremely brazen face and an expression that you see frequently on half-educated people who turn their heads into dumps of half-read and half-understood brochures, pamphlets, and proclamations.

"Get dressed, Boitsov. You're under arrest!" I said to him.

"By what authority, if I may ask?"

"No authority. You're under arrest, and that's it!"

"It doesn't work like that, so would you please be so kind to tell me which article of the 1903 criminal code provides basis for my arrest?"

"Stop it with the criminal code! I am the chief of detective police, I suspect you of fraud, and I think it necessary to arrest you. Is that clear?"

"That's sheer lawlessness, bureaucratic ways, outrageous violence!"

I summoned two policemen, and Boitsov was taken to the police station. There he kept on behaving defiantly and brazenly. He denied any guilt, protesting again the arrest was illegal, and asked to immediately give him a sheet of paper to write a complaint to the public prosecutor.

"What kind of sheet: a big one or a small one?" I asked with irony.

"Doesn't matter!" he replied dryly.

"You may write to the prosecutor; you have the right to do so. But maybe you will also recall what happened to the appropriation ticket for 10,000 rubles that had your handwriting on the counterfoil? You know, there's an odd thing about it. The ticket with this number has never been submitted to the Governorate Treasury."

This evidence, however, didn't daunt the impudent man.

"How am I supposed to remember all the tickets? Even if there was a mistake or confusion of some kind, after all, it doesn't mean you can just lock people up like this!"

After 24 hours of Boitsov's fruitless detention, I again called for Leontiev.

"I guess, Leontiev, you're going to have to be locked up for a couple of days."

"Well, sir, I guess I am. It's not like it's the first time."

"Right, but this time you'll have to deal with it very delicately. Boitsov is an old stager. If there's a slightest hiccup, he'll sense it, and the whole deal will be ruined!"

"I'll do my best, sir!"

"Here's the thing: I think the best way for you to do it will be to attack him with swearing and reproaches, blaming him for your arrest. Refer to your recent meeting at the tavern and to the fact that he and everyone he met had been kept under surveillance. Do you understand?"

"Yes, sir!"

Leontiev played his part perfectly. According to what my agents eavesdropped and his later report, it was as I said: As soon as Leontiev was put in a cell and saw Boitsov in it, he attacked him and started to swear at him right away.

"You, bastard! Damn you! Why am I supposed to suffer because of some scum? I just got a good job, and there it is. Now I'm gonna lose everything because of a piece of s-- like you! It's you who's responsible for all the filthy business you do, so why do you draw honest people into it, damn you?"

Disconcerted, Boitsov was saying something, trying to justify himself and calm down his raging companion.

"What're you yelling about? How come it's my fault?"

"How come?" Leontiev angrily mimicked. "Because. If you know you've done something wrong, don't even get close to people in the street. It's not like you're an innocent, so I guess you knew cops were watching you, dumbass."

"What are you talking about? I didn't do anything wrong, and I had no idea they were watching me!"

"Right, keep talking, play the innocent! You must have gained a lot, or maybe even killed someone! I couldn't even think about it."

After scolding like this for about an hour, Leontiev was tired and fell asleep.

Two days passed. On the third day, Leontiev said he was going to "take a leak" and headed to my office.

"So, how's it going?" I asked him.

"That was hard, sir! For two days he was standing firm, but then, he finally trusted me. It was three hours ago when he asked me to do something. He said,

'You will be freed soon probably, so please do me a favor. Go to my aunt. She lives at the house of the university president's assistant and works there as a cook. Tell her that if she's called to police, she has to keep silent about me being her nephew and having visited her recently. If you do the favor, I will give you the address of a good pal of mine, and I will give you a note for him, so he will pay you 25 rubles. And if you carry that out well, you'll get 25 more. I have helped him when he was in trouble many times, so he wouldn't refuse me that money.'

'Okay,' I said, 'fifty rubles is good money. But how will I take your note out of here, if they search everyone at the exit?'

'Oh, that's nothing! The note is very small, put it somewhere, like in your armpit, or in your mouth.'"

"Great, Leontiev! Go visit the old lady immediately."

Leontiev went there and did what he was asked to do. When talking to the old woman, he also added that she mustn't tell anyone about that thing that her nephew left her at his last visit.

The next day I summoned the old woman to the police. She came with her five-year-old granddaughter. She was an ancient lady, looking around eighty-years old, but still quite lively. Before she even heard my question, she started jabbering like a trained parrot:

"I don't know anyone named Andrei Boitsov, and a person named that never came to my place and didn't bring anything with him."

The little girl whispered:

"Grandma, why are you saying that Uncle Andrei didn't come, when he stopped by recently?"

I grabbed the little girl and took her to another room. I gave her some caramels and asked:

"When did Uncle Andrei come to you?"

The girl was scared and remained silent for a long while, but them calmed down and told me that Uncle Andrei stopped by recently and gave a bundle to her grandma.

"Where did your grandma put the bundle?"

"I don't know," she replied. There was nothing else she could tell me.

I took her back to my office.

"Don't listen to her, good sir. She's just a child, an angel of God!" the old lady sweetly babbled, and them threatened the girl with a fist and angrily uttered, "You little brat, I'll show you!"

"Shame on you, ma'am! You already have one foot in the grave, and yet you're taking such a sin upon your soul! You probably should know that your nephew killed a man with a knife, robbed him, and brought the money to you to hide it! The girl told me that you had the bundle."

"What are you saying, good sir, good heavens! Would I ever be pleasing a murderer like this? It's just that the child is silly. She'll tell you all kinds of things! No, before the Holy One above I'm telling you, I'm innocent, innocent, innoce-e-ent!"

I was afraid of what the old lady could do because of her anger, so I myself took the girl to the university president's assistant's place, passed her over to him, told him about the whole deal, and asked him to protect the girl as well as try to persuade the old lady as far as he could to give up the things she had hidden.

The search we conducted at the old lady's room resulted in nothing, which didn't surprise me much, since she could have hidden the things in the university's attic that stretched along the top of the building for over a thousand feet.

The case was deadlocked, and I couldn't see a thread to catch at. The search at the place of Boitsov's pal, who gave Leontiev 25 rubles based on the note, was fruitless too.

Since I had nothing better to do, I had to resort to a rather questionable method.

I called for Leontiev and told him that he would have to "go to prison" again. The story was that he was been arrested again after getting into an ambush that was laid for him at the old woman's place when he came there to do what Boitsov had asked him about.

"Now, Leontiev, your part is even more difficult. So try hard not to fail!"

In fifteen minutes Leontiev was already yelling for people in all the cells to hear:

"Damn you and your damn money! What a fool I was to listen to you and go to that freaking witch, damn her! That's it, I'm done, got into this mess! Why the hell did I do this?! Got tempted by fifty rubles? Well, there you go now. I lost the job, stained myself, and God knows how this will even end! Get away from me, you bastard!" he screamed in full cry to Boitsov, who came up to him to console him.

Boitsov bought it again and spoke in half-whispering voice:

"No need to be so upset. Lost your job? That's nothing! As soon as we get out of here, I can assure you, there'll be enough for both of us. But you have to help me till the end, and you won't be down."

"Sure, right, keep talking! Like everyone who deals with you isn't down. I'll get into a mess again because of you. First cops saw me with you in the tavern, then I got to this ambush at your aunt's place. I guess there's no more good luck for me out there."

Boitsov was consoling Leontiev for a long time. Soon I called the latter for "interrogation."

When Leontiev came back to the cell after the interrogation, he was considerably calmer.

"Well, thank God, I think I really threw some dust in their eyes! I said I got to your aunt's place by mistake when I was trying to get to the treasurer's apartment—one girl I know really got a housemaid job there a little while ago. I think they bought it. They promised to check it, and told me that if it was true, they would let me go right away. So let them check, 'cause that girl really works there, and I gave them her last name."

When Leontiev was about to be freed again, in about three days, Boitsov asked him for another favor:

"Go to 10 Chernyshevsky Lane. My uncle lives there and works as a doorman. Tell him that Andrei was arrested and asks him to hide the coat that I gave him very well. 'Cause I don't know how long I will have to stay here, and I am worried about the coat. You know, moths can eat it."

Leontiev angrily told him to go to hell.

"Is all my trouble because of you not enough? No, brother, you stay here, and I'm done! I've walked around your relatives' places a lot. I'm not doing it anymore."

I went to Chernyshevsky Lane to the indicated building with a few agents and asked the sprightly doorman:

"Where is Andrei Boitsov?"

"I don't know, Your Most Honorable Sir," the doorman answered, lifting his cap a little bit.

"Where's the coat he left here?"

"He left a coat. It's right here. I put it under my head last night."

"Give it!"

"Sure, here you go."

We ripped up the lining and discovered a layer of 500-ruble bills.

We counted them: There were 250,000 rubles. When the doorman saw it, he went pale with surprise.

"Damn, I didn't see that coming!" he said slowly, scratching the back of his head.

As soon as we got back to the police department, I was suddenly informed that the old cook had come to see me.

"Your Most Honorable Sir, please forgive me, I was a fool. My master moved me so much with his speeches, that I decided to come and confess. I don't want to take a sin upon my soul! I brought you Andriushka's[23] bundle, please have it."

To my great surprise, wrapped in the bundle were not 50,000 rubles, but 58,000.

It turned out afterwards that there was a mistake in the treasury, and instead of 300,000, they gave him 308,000 rubles.

I invited magistrate R. and district court prosecutor Brun de Saint-Ippolite to my office, put 58,000 rubles on my desk and covered them with a newspaper, sat at the desk, and laid the "stuffed" coat near my feet. Then I called for Boitsov.

He showed up as usual, extremely cheeky, and immediately inquired about the title of the person present whom he didn't know, Mr. Brun.

"He is the court prosecutor," I replied.

"Mister Prosecutor, I ask for your intervention! It's been a week since I was arrested for no reason and kept locked up. This is no good; there are no laws for that! The criminal code says that—"

"See that?" I took the newspaper away and showed the money under it.

He wasn't confused.

"So what? You put some public money on your desk, and you think you can catch me out?"

"Now see that?" I lifted the coat above my head.

---

[23] Andriushka is a diminutive for Andrei

Boitsov went crimson and pronounced:

"Well, now this is something. This is real, legal, physical evidence!" He hung his head and fell into gloomy silence.

According to an Imperial order, 10,000 rubles were given as a reward to the police officials who worked on this outstanding case.

A Lost Russian Soul (Vasya Whitetache)

I am somewhat agitated now, as I begin the story of criminal adventures of Vasya Whitetache, who ended his turbulent odyssey on the gibbet.

Thousands of criminals of the most diverse shades had marched before me within my many years of service, but this single rebellious life, this lost soul stands alone in the gloomy gallery of my anti-heroes. Everything about this man was outstanding, from his unique, if I may say, criminal ethics, to his exceptionally courageous acceptance of death.

But I'm not going to rush, and I will tell the story as it unfolded.

In 1911 an epidemic of armed robberies broke out in a region near Moscow. A common feature for all of the robberies was a specific humanity that the robbers displayed. Although victims would be cleaned out, sometimes tied up and sometimes locked in closets, bathrooms and other secluded parts of the places being robbed, they would never be killed or even injured. It was like the robbers had an aversion to shedding human blood. There were several dozens of robberies and larcenies like that, but the district police's searches produced no results.

The Moscow police was responsible only for defending the territory of the city, but due to the unsuccessful performance of the district police, the Governor of Moscow Province, General Dzhunkovsky, asked me to help them as far as we could.

Our efforts weren't any more successful in the beginning. The robbers consistently managed to escape our searches. None of the raids led to catching the gang or its leader. In fact, it was the leader who was the mainspring of the entire affair. Apparently, he didn't have a settled number of accomplices, a conclusion drawn from the different number of participants in each single case.

After arresting one of the robbers who tarried at the crime scene, as well as after collecting rumors in nearby villages, we learned that the leader of the gang was a certain Vasily Belousov, nicknamed Vasya Whitetache[24].

What we heard about him was rather curious: he kept his hands off paupers (although there was nothing to take away from them anyway) and directed his efforts to well-off people. After a successful robbery, he would go on a spree and throw about stolen money in nearby villages with a generous hand that knew no limits. He would buy meals and drinks for everyone around and shower his fellow villagers and neighbors with gifts, pleasing everyone who happened to be within reach of his generous hand. Of course, this exactly was the explanation of Vasya's long elusiveness. Peasants readily sheltered this person who was so kind to them and brought them so much benefit.

Whitetache's biography is as follows: A foundling with no kith and kin, he was picked up and raised by a tenderhearted old woman. Since he was a child, he displayed humility and industry. First, he was a shepherd in the village, and he became an excellent worker. Finally, after soldiering, he went back to his homeland and got a job with one of the local rich men. That was the time when he first met Vasily the Pocked, his fellow villager, a local blacksmith, the greatest of scum and a drunkard everybody loathed. I believe that the blacksmith's influence was fatal to Whitetache.

It was less than six months later when the blacksmith convinced Vasily to rob their master. In the course of the robbery, the blacksmith insisted they kill him, and it was only Whitetache's resistance that saved their master from death.

---

[24] The surname 'Belousov' comes from Russian words *belyi*, meaning 'white', and *us* (pronounced *oos*), meaning 'moustache'

Their master was so scared that he kept silence for a long time, but the case was eventually solved. The blacksmith was sentenced to four years of penal battalions. Whitetache was sentenced to one and a half years. The time he spent in prison was not a time of idleness. He developed the rudiments of literacy that he had acquired during soldiering and learned to read swiftly and write calligraphically. Apparently, as it will be evident as this story goes further, he randomly chose books of a certain kind that developed a sort of romanticism in him, which must have been inherent in him since he was born. The one-sided development of his imagination and the pernicious effect of prison, which always leaves an imprint on people who are impressionable to any extent—these two factors once and for all threw Whitetache to the path of criminal adventures. After serving his term of imprisonment, Vasya ran wild, which was the reason for my intervention.

Bloodless robberies followed back-to-back. Some thieves would be caught on spot, some during dealing in stolen things. But Vasya Whitetache escaped every time. Several times during raids, policemen fired at him, but never successfully, and Vasya used the peasants' protection to disappear without a trace. Catching him was also difficult because there was only one person in the police who knew Vasya by sight—Muratov, who came from the same village as Vasya.

After a series of successful robberies, Vasya began to bombard me with letters. It was hard to say what his motives were to do so: He either liked to play with fire, or wanted to tease people who were hunting for him, or maybe he blindly believed he was almighty, invulnerable, and infinitely lucky.

Thus he wrote:

"The affair in such-and-such place is the doing of me, Vasya Whitetache, a famous leader of the uncatchable gang, who was born under the lucky star of Stenka Razin[25]. I do not shed human blood, but I'm having my share of freedom and doing what I want. Don't try to catch me—I'm uncatchable. Neither fire nor bullets stop me. A spell has been cast over me."

---

[25] Stenka Razin was the leader of a major uprising against the tsarist regime in Russia in 1670-1671

However, soon Vasya's robberies' pattern changed. Officer Belyanchikov was killed on Vladimir Road. The next day I received a letter:

"His Honor, mister officer Belyanchikov, was killed by me, Vasya Whitetache. He was pressing us too hard, and threw glances at Pasha. I didn't rob him, only took his revolver, because why would he need it now? It will come in handy to us, though."

In a few days, near the Lyubertsy station, a post captain's widow was killed and robbed.

Vasya wrote:

"It was me, Vasya Whitetache, who robbed the general's wife in Lyubertsy. Her insults made me kill her."

In a few more days, the house of a family of peasants was robbed. A 14-year-old daughter of the owner was raped by one of the robbers.

That same day a dead body was found near the village where the robbery had taken place.

Vasya's letter read:

"I committed the robbery in such-and-such village, and I shot Petya Shagov down myself: I don't do rape."

Since robberies now were accompanied by murders, I made the entire police force extend themselves. But Vasya Whitetache still wasn't caught.

He was finally seized in accidental and extremely tragic circumstances.

One day, early in the morning, my inspector Muratov (as I said, he was the only one of my agents who knew Vasya by sight) went to a marketplace with his wife to shop. Suddenly he noticed Vasya in the crowd. He knew how feverishly eager the police were in their searches for this most dangerous criminal, so Muratov, without thinking much, dashed to him, and, despite being unarmed and also a rather feeble man, he seized the colossus by the arm and started screaming for help. Vasya shook poor Muratov off with one movement of his mighty shoulder, drew his Browning, and fired twice point-blank. Mortally wounded, Muratov fell down, bleeding. Some people ran up to him, but this hero of duty, still conscious, worriedly groaned:

"Leave me! My game is over. Get him, get him quickly, Vasya Whitetache!"

Meanwhile Vasya rushed through the marketplace, ran up to a fence and started climbing over it. A boy who was around and got infected by the crowd's enthusiasm in trying to catch Vasya, dug his teeth into Vasya's leg as the latter was climbing and hung on, holding as firm as possible. Policemen ran up to the fence, seized the brigand, disarmed him and took him to the nearest police station.

I was immediately notified by the phone, and went there right away. Muratov's body had been transported to that police station, too. I looked at Vasya without saying anything and was about to leave, when suddenly he said to me:

"Mister Chief, please order for me to be transferred to your station. I need to talk to you."

I didn't reply, turned around, and left. However, I gave the command to transfer Vasya.

Poor Muratov was killed by two shots in his chest. I felt very sad when two days later I followed the coffin of my courageous colleague, and I felt even sadder when I saw the tears of his widow and his children, now fatherless. I bore indignation in my soul when I was about to start interrogating Muratov's killer, but as soon as he appeared in my office and said his first words, the feeling of anger began to quieten down inside me, giving place to some sort of curiosity first, and then, I guess, to the feeling (may deceased Muratov forgive me for it!) of some kind of liking.

It is commonly thought that a villain responsible for a series of murders must inevitably reflect this God's curse, this mark of Cain, in his appearance. In reality that is not true. Degenerative characteristics are found among inveterate lawbreakers as frequently as regular characters, and quite a lot of villains are people of pleasant and even friendly appearance, with a humble, likeable smile and quite often with an innocent, childlike expression in their almost angelic eyes.

Vasya Whitetache was one of these latter ones. He was a handsome man of the stature and build of an epic hero, very tidy and, if you will, elegant in his own way. His appearance was positively charming. A proudly set, fair-haired head with a pleasant face, big grey eyes, an aquiline nose and thick, furry mustache—that's what he looked like. He walked into my office wearing a long tight coat thrown on his mighty shoulder, tall blacked boots, and steel handcuffs. He definitely looked like a daredevil from an old Russian heroic epic.

This impression was so strong that, unexpectedly to myself, I fell into a sort of epic tone as I spoke.

"Well, Vasya, you've had your share of freedom, and now it's over. Time to face the music! Don't try to lie to me, tell everything as your conscience tells you to, and don't you hide anything in the depth of your soul."

"You're right, mister chief. I won't hide a thing; I'll tell you everything. The fellow did what he did, and now's the time for the fellow to pay."

"So why, Vasya, did you write all those letters? Saying you didn't shed any blood, while in reality—how many souls have perished because of you?"

"No, mister chief, what I wrote was all true: I haven't shed a single drop of blood for nothing, neither have I ever let any of my companions do so."

"What about the police officer, the widow in Lyubertsy, and Shagov?"

"Those weren't for nothing. I shot down mister officer because he was troubling Pasha with his filthy offers. I love my Pasha more than life. And concerning the general's wife in Lyubertsy, I have to admit, that was a bad thing I did. I didn't want to kill her, but I couldn't endure it."

"What couldn't you endure?"

"How could I, mister chief? We got into her apartment at night. I went to the bedroom, she was there, asleep. I took the watch and the ring from her bedside table, but it was so dark, I hit a carafe with water in it, then—bang!—it fell on the floor. The woman woke up, sprang up, got mad, and jumped at me, and punched me in the face, and then again … I couldn't endure such insult, so I killed her for that. I didn't want to kill her, I actually fired just to scare her, but unfortunately enough I hit her in a fatal spot."

"What about Shagov?"

"That guy got what he deserved. Don't do rape, and don't brag about it. I don't want Vasya Whitetache to have ill fame, for he isn't a murderer or a rapist! He doesn't make people suffer for nothing."

"Let it be, Vasya, let it be as you say. But what about Muratov, my poor Muratov, why didn't you spare him? Look at you. You're broad as an ox, and Muratov was a weak, feeble man. Besides, he was unarmed. You could've pushed him, or shook him off yourself. Why did you need to kill him?"

Vasya gave a deep sigh.

"Yes, mister chief, I admit, what I did to him was mean. I don't even know what it was that came over me. I just looked at him, and I became so angry. I was afraid to lose my dear freedom, too. So without thinking much, I just drew it and fired. Now I'm bitter when I remember this. Please allow me, mister chief, to see his wife and his children. I will throw myself at their feet and beg them to forgive me!"

"Yes, you will, but what's the point? You won't resurrect the dead!"

"You're right!" Vasya said and gave a deeper sigh.

I thought for a while and said:

"Vasya, things look black for you. The security in Moscow Governorate is increased now, and Belyanchikov was a public officer, so I don't think you'll escape the gallows!"

"Well, mister chief, I guess that will be the right thing. People like me should be hung by law. Fellows like us only bring harm and trouble, and no good."

"I feel sorry for you though, Vasya. Here you are, repenting and not denying anything, but I'm afraid I can't help you, no matter how much I intercede for you."

"Don't you try to intercede, mister chief. There is no need. That would be in vain. If they send me to hard labor, I will escape and get back to business. Once a man comes to the end of the line, there's no way he can stop. That's over. No matter how much you please him, he'll still long for evil. No, mister chief! I thank you very much, but don't bother yourself, don't intercede, don't stain your soul like that. I should be hung, and I will accept my end without repining. There's only one thing I ask you. I will tell you everything, without hiding anything, and I will give you the names of all the scum that's been at work with me, hang them, kill them, exterminate them, for without me, without my hold, they will go wild and do things that will heat the heavens up!

But there's one thing, mister chief, I am telling you before the Holy One above, and you may believe me or not, but my Pasha wasn't part of any evil of mine. Please don't doubt it, and don't arrest her."

At this moment an inspector informed me quietly that some young girl had come to the detective police, said her name was Pasha, and asked to be arrested and put in jail with Belousov.

"Send her in!" I said.

The inspector left.

"Pasha has come," I said to Vasya.

"I knew she would. She loves me!" he replied with a tinge of pride.

The door opened, and a girl, a Gypsy by appearance, timidly entered my office. Matte skin, coral lips, enormous black eyes.

She was almost just a kid. For some reason she reminded me one of bronze figurines of Indian dancers. When she saw Whitetache, she forgot about everything and threw herself at him. The colossus was about to stretch his arms, wishing to embrace her, but his steel handcuffs stopped him. He gnashed his teeth with vexation, tried to break his fetters with a violent move, then doubled up and put his face

174

out to Pasha. Her small head sank into his furry mustache, and her arms twined around the neck that leaned down toward her.

In an instant, he felt ashamed about his impulse, drew himself up, tenderly pushed Pasha aside and said to her:

"You see, Pasha, who you fell in love with?" he held the handcuffs out to her.

Pasha started crying and pressed herself to him.

"Ah, Vasya, does it even matter? I want to be with you, in prison, or even in hard labor!"

"No, Pasha. My end has come. I've had my share of doing what I wanted, but it's over. It won't be hard labor that I'll be granted, but a noose and a crosspiece!"

Pasha started crying even louder.

"And if you really love me the way you say, then there's no need for you to feed lice in prison. Instead, go to a nunnery and pray to God for forgiveness of my dreadful sins till the end of your life!"

I was moved and upset, so I let Vasya and Pasha go to a cell. This man's confession, his tone, the way he behaved, and, finally, this touching love shook my nerves. I had no doubt that Vasya was genuine and far from any kind of pose or affectation.

The following two weeks, which Vasya spent at the detective police, proved it. He was meek, polite, humble, and thoughtful, as if he was preparing for death, solemnly expecting the formidable hour.

Sometimes he'd be asked, "Vasya, do you maybe want some vodka or something else?"

He'd say, "Thank you very much, mister chief. It's not the time for vodka now. It's a different time, a time to think about the soul."

It was a bright spring day, full of life, shining, and joy, when Vasya was taken out of our building to the street under escort to be transferred to prison. I was standing by the open window of my office and observed that sad sight. Vasya came out without a hat, rising above the crowd, a head taller than anyone around. He was walking sedately, slowly, and as he came up to the prison carriage, he turned to everybody, bowed from the waist, and loudly said:

"Forgive me, my brothers, for I am a sinner!" Then he got into the carriage, and it took off.

I fell into deep pensiveness and sympathy. In spite of all his crimes, Vasya wasn't detestable to me. I was thinking: If this man had been raised in other circumstances, if he had grown in a different environment, if he had enlightened his mind with nourishing knowledge, he would've become a great soul instead of a criminal soul. For some reason, I believed that this was exactly the kind of dough that nature used to model big personalities, and in this case the dough chosen for him was rich and good, but there had been either a lack of yeast or a lack of kindling, so the dough went sour before it even rose.

Vasily's death was astonishing.

I wasn't present at his execution, but the prosecutor's friend C. told me about it with a tremor in his voice and tears in his eyes:

"So he was brought to the execution venue. Vasily was absolutely calm.

He loudly confessed and repented his sins from the bottom of his heart.

After the confession, he said to me, 'Your Honor, may I say a couple of words to the soldiers?'

Although that's not permitted, I decided to make an exception. Vasily turned to the guards of the escort and said:

'Brothers! All the politicians say that hanging people is unacceptable, that government has no right to do that, that a human being is not a dog or anything and so on. They're wrong! A person like me is worse than a dog. If I'm not hanged, a lot of innocent blood will be shed again. So listen to your higher-ups; they know best.'

Then Belousov turned to me again:

'Your Honor, please allow me not to put the sack on my head.'

I could hardly stand on my feet, so I could only nod my approval.

Vasily approached the gallows, got on the stool himself, waved to the executioner who was coming up to him to stop, and said:

'Don't sully your hands. I'll do it myself.'

After that he unbuttoned the collar of his shirt, threw the noose on his neck, fixed it, gave a deep sigh, raised his eyes to the morning's sky, and quietly whispered:

'Goodbye, Pasha!'

Then he screwed up his eyelids tightly, pushed the stool away with a strong blow, and hung by the noose. A few cramps in his body, a few convulsions in his fingers, and he became quiet forever.

The gendarmerie officer was crying, the guards were crying, and I ...."

Pasha followed Vasily's precept precisely. She took herself off to Novodevichy Convent, where under the heavy vaults of the holy abode she began her prayers for forgiveness of the bloody sins of her dead lover.

The Theft at a Kharkov Bank

This case especially is engraved on my memory, possibly due to the fact that it closed the period of my many years of service to the Russian Empire.

It is also memorable because the amount stolen from the bank was so large that the history of banks in Russia had known no similar cases.

So, on December 28, 1916, i.e., two months before the revolution, when I already was the head of all of the police of the Empire, I received a cipher text from the assistant chair of the Kharkov Police, Mr. Lapsin, who informed me about a theft from the Kharkov Bank of the Salesmen Society of Mutual Credit. Stolen were interest-bearing securities for 2,500,000 rubles and a comparatively insignificant amount of cash. Lapsin said that the thieves had dug a tunnel from the yard of the house next to the bank, entered the bank's steel room through it, and used certain instruments that he, Lapsin, had never seen before to saw and solder steel safes open and take the mentioned valuables from them. No traces of the thieves were found, but one of the bank's employees was detained and temporarily arrested as he was suspected of complicity in the crime. I received the telegram in the morning, at about eleven, and at four the Director of the Police Department A. T. Vasiliev told me that the Minister for Internal Affairs had just reported to the Emperor and announced that His Majesty had read about the Kharkov theft in the morning newspaper and expressed his will to see this crime solved as soon as possible. That is why the Minister found it necessary to assign this case to me.

I couldn't leave immediately, since the Kharkov express had already departed, so I postponed my trip till the next day, December 29.

This brazen theft worried me in every possible way. Aside from the exceptionally large amount of stolen money that drew even the attention of the Emperor, the case's circumstances didn't provide certainty in the success of my searches. The thing was that the thieves had taken advantage of the Christmas holidays, i.e., the two days when the bank was closed. Therefore, there had been 48 hours between the time the crime was committed and the time it was revealed.

Within this period of time, the thieves could have thoroughly covered their tracks or maybe even left the country.

The general picture of the crime made me think that the people at work here were the so-called "Warsaw thieves."

Thieves of this type were not quite ordinary, and they were dramatically different from Russian thieves. "Warsaw thieves" share a few characteristics: They are always well-dressed and live richly, staying only at first-class hotels and eating their meals at first-class restaurants. When planning a theft, they do not squander their talents on trifles, i.e., they always choose significant valuables as the target of their work.

Preparing an affair costs them a lot of money. They widely practice bribery and employ the most perfected and expensive of instruments, which they leave at the scene of the crime.

They are diligent, persistent, and patient. They are always well-armed.

If they are caught, they do not deny their guilt and calmly testify about everything, but they do not give up their accomplices.

Among two million photos of dactylographic prints and marks that had been collected at the department from criminals and suspects, there was a special series of photos for "Warsaw thieves." I took about twenty photos of especially artful and brazen thieves from this series with me to Kharkov, just in case.

The quite talented agent Linder accepted my invitation to accompany me. He was a young man, a native of Poland, who, among other things, possessed a true gift of imitating all kinds of foreign accents when speaking Russian. He was particularly good at doing Jews and Finns.

So, on December 29, Linder and I departed to Kharkov and, due to the train's delay, arrived there on the evening of December 31st.

I immediately summoned Lapsin, and he told me the details of the matter. Basically, he retold the content of his cipher text and added the grounds for arresting the bank employee. It turned out that the tunnel had been being dug from a woodshed in the yard of a house occupied by this bank employee. This gentleman's reputation generally wasn't good. When the theft was carried out, he was out of town. He and his wife had left for two days, to a place near Kharkov. But despite of this alibi, the judicial investigator found it necessary to arrest him, since the digging of the tunnel had certainly taken two weeks at least and had been going on right by the wall of this official's apartment, so it seemed impossible that the knocking of pickaxes and shovels hadn't been noticed by him.

On the next day, I decided to examine the crime scene myself.

The examination of the tunnel confirmed the investigator's assumptions.

Concerning the bank's steel room, it was a very curious thing to see. Two safes with walls almost seven inches thick were mutilated and opened as if with projectiles. Scattered all over the room were some highly-perfected instruments for breaking in: electric saws, gas cylinders, cans with acid, some sophisticated drills and accumulators, and batteries. In short, the instruments left there must have cost several thousand rubles.

The official I interrogated turned out to be a Pole who denied everything and protested against the arrest, which he claimed was illegal.

Since digging the tunnel and preparation for the theft must have taken quite a while, the thieves, I thought, had been living in Kharkov for a certain period of time. That is why I took Linder and a

180

few local agents and started inspecting hotels, having twenty photos of Warsaw thieves with me and the photo of the arrested official.

I was lucky. In one hotel, out of about ten we visited, staff members recognized two professional thieves, Stanisław Kwiatkowski and Zdzisław Goroszek., and in another one—Jan Sandaewski and three more people, whose names I do not remember. There were six people overall. It turned out those people had been living in the hotels for about a month and left on December 26.

I also learned something else new. The arrested official was recognized by a footman of the hotel where Kwiatkowski and Goroszek were staying. Not only did this footman, a lively fellow, recognize both thieves and the official, but he also, giggling, told me about a certain curious story that he had been a part of during those gentlemen's stay in his hotel. According to him, the arrested official would stop by Goroszek's room frequently, and even more often by Kwiatkowski's room; moreover, Kwiatkowski apparently had an intimate connection with the wife of the official, who had no idea. This woman visited Kwiatkowski in the hotel many times, and he, the footman, repeatedly was assigned to pass little notes from him to her or the other way around. The footman was apparently familiar with those secret notes' content and was thus convinced, to his amusement, of their connection.

I had the feeling that this day, the first day of the New Year, was not wasted, so I went to sleep in peace.

Meanwhile, additional information we had collected about the arrested official didn't favor him. Before Kharkov, he worked in Helsingfors[26], in a branch office of Crédit Lyonnais, where he was fired based on suspicion of complicity in preparation for a theft in this bank.

My further interrogations of the arrested official resulted in nothing. He kept denying any guilt. After giving it a lot of thinking, I decided to try the following.

"Here's the deal." I said to Linder. "You should move immediately to another hotel far from me, and tomorrow go to the

---

[26] Helsingfors is another name for Helsinki

arrested official's wife and tell her that you're friends with Kwiatkowski and that you're about to leave Kharkov, so you stopped by to give his regards to her. For more credibility, show her Kwiatkowski's photo as if he had given it to you with a friendly message written on the back of it. You do the message in Polish. We have a copy of his handwriting in his file, use it as an example. We really want to receive a letter or a note addressed to Kwiatkowski from this woman."

Linder carried the plan out brilliantly. The next day the woman received him. This is what he told me about this visit:

"'I have come to you, Pani, from Stasik[27] Kwiatkowski, a good friend of mine. Pan Stanisław asked me to send his regards and to say he misses Pani cordially.'

'Ja nie rozumiem, co pan mówi[28],' she said confusedly. 'Who is Pan Stanisław, who is Pan Kwiatkowski?'

I indulgently smiled.

'Pani is very scared! So for you not to be worried, Stasik asked me to show this portrait to Pani. Would you be so kind?' I held the photo with a message out to her.

After glancing at it, the woman beamed with joy, calmed down, and suddenly became friendlier.

'Ah, please, please, dear Pan, have a seat!'

Then everything went very smoothly. She confessed to me that she had been missing Kwiatkowski very much, and she put me in a difficult situation by consistently asking where Pan Stanisław was now. I found a way out of it by pleading women's tendency to talk.

'Pan Stanisław, as much as he loves you and trusts you, asked me to not give you his address, for he is worried that you might let out this secret. Because if this were to happen, the entire affair carried out by him and your husband might be ruined.'

---

[27] Stasik is a diminutive of Stanisław.

[28] I do not understand what you are talking about (Polish).

'Oh, Pan Stanisław really shouldn't doubt me! For his sake, and for my husband's sake, and for my own sake after all, I must be careful. Although, let it be the way he wants!'"

Overall, Linder was received very warmly, served a delicious dinner, and in the evening, as he was leaving the hospitable hostess, he said nonchalantly:

"Maybe Pani wishes to write something to Stasik. I will gladly pass your cedulka[29] to him."

Pani was glad about this opportunity and immediately wrote an affectionate message to Kwiatkowski, concluding it with the phrase, "What a pity, beloved Stasik, that you're not with me now that my husband is in prison!"

I thanked Linder for the well-accomplished assignment and summoned the arrested official on the next day.

"So, will you keep denying your participation in the affair?"

"Certainly!"

"And will you deny your acquaintance with Kwiatkowski?"

"I don't know anyone named like that."

"So your wife doesn't know Pan Kwiatkowski either?"

"Of course not. Who is that Kwiatkowski person?"

"Your wife's lover!"

"Oh, you know what? This trick won't work! My wife is a saint, and I believe in her fidelity as much as I believe in the fact that I'm breathing."

"Well, you shouldn't. For I can prove otherwise."

"Nonsense. Even if I admit the inadmissible conjuncture of my wife cheating on me with Kwiatkowski, how could you possibly

---

[29] A note (Polish)

prove it to me? You haven't witnessed her with Pan Stanisław yourself, have you?"

"How come you know his name?"

The official was very confused, but then came to his senses and replied:

"You called Kwiatkowski that at one of the interrogations."

"I don't remember that. Your memory must be outstanding! But let's drop it and speak seriously. I have a special offer for you. I promise I will prove to you, as simply as two plus two is four, that your wife is unfaithful, and you will help me to find Kwiatkowski, who has stained your family honor. Deal?"

"No, not a deal! Because I do not know Kwiatkowski, so I cannot help you find him. But I'm telling you that I won't spare my wife's lover, if there turned out to be one."

"Okay. Such promise is good enough. I suppose you know your wife's handwriting well?"

"Of course!"

"Then please take and read this. It's a letter she wrote yesterday and addressed to Stanisław Kwiatkowski." I held out to him the sealed pink envelope that Linder had given me.

The official grasped the envelope, opened it, took the sheet of paper out of it and started to read it avidly. I observed him. As he read, his face turned crimson, his hands started shaking and he breathed heavily. When he finished, he crumpled the paper in wrath, threw a mad look, banged his fist on the desk and exclaimed:

"Psia krew![30] Pan Stanisław, you won't come back to this city soon. And if you do, it won't be to meet my wife. That bastard, that scum! I'll show you! If I go down, I'll take you with me! Sir," he said to me, "please ask me now. I will tell everything, everything now. I'll be glad to help you catch this rat Kwiatkowski!"

---

[30] Literally: dog's blood (Polish)

"Okay. Where is he now?"

"He must be in Moscow, at the place of Goroszek's lover, on Pereyaslavlskaya Street."

"Does he have the stolen things with him?"

"Yes, he does. He is planning to exchange the interest bearing securities for money and then divide it between all the participants."

"Maybe he has already exchanged them and divided?"

"No. It's not that easy. Kwiatkowski and Goroszek are extremely careful. A certain 'dealer' named Hämäläinen is supposed to come from Helsingfors to Kharkov for the exchange. I know him personally. He will receive a reference letter from me here in Kharkov, and then go to Moscow to buy the securities for about a half of their nominal price."

"Can you write this letter now, sign it and address it to Kwiatkowski?"

"I am very eager to do that!"

"Very well! Here is an envelope and paper."

In about ten minutes, the letter was written, signed and addressed to Kwiatkowski , on Pereyaslavlskaya St. in Moscow.

"Here's the letter; do it!" the official rubbed his hands in joy. "Well, Pan Stanisław, here it comes. Every dog has its day!"

The official frankly confessed to his participation in the affair. He provided the woodshed for digging the tunnel and promised to summon Hämäläinen from Helsingfors. Also, he gave us the names of all the participants of the "enterprise." Together with Kwiatkowski and Goroszek, there were nine of them.

I immediately sent the photos of five thieves recognized in Kharkov hotels to the chief of the Moscow police, Mr. Marschalk (who had taken my place), and asked him to make an effort to find three of them first of all and set up careful surveillance over Kwiatkowski and Goroszek in Pereyaslavlskaya St.

I called for Linder, told him about the official's confession, and added:

"From now on, Linder, you are not Linder, but Hämäläinen!"

"Sirty kopeks, perkjärvi, kuokkala![31]" he replied, making the impassive, sleepy face of a Finn.

I couldn't help bursting out laughing.

Due to his frank confession and assistance to the investigation, I ordered that the imprisonment of the arrested official be mitigated to a reasonable extent. He was allowed to receive food from home, accept visitors, go for walks, sleep on a separate bed with sheets, etc. But at the same time, I talked to the head of Kharkov prison and emphasized the significance of the arrested man's crime, as it had drawn the attention of the Emperor. Therefore, notwithstanding all the measures of mitigation, I ordered that they set up the strictest isolation for the arrested official, that they inspect most thoroughly his parcels, etc. I thought my job in Kharkov was completed, so Linder and I left for Petrograd. All the way there, Linder practiced his Finnish accent, so by the time we reached the capital he had practically achieved perfection.

On our way from Kharkov, I caught a cold, so I couldn't depart for Moscow right away. Meanwhile the matter brooked no delay, so I sent L. A. Kurnatowski to replace me temporarily. Kurnatowski was the former chief of the Warsaw police. After the Warsaw evacuation, he was assigned to the department of police and thus came under my command. I knew him as quite an artful and bright functionary. Linder went to Moscow with Kurnatowski to play the part of Hämäläinen from Helsingfors there. At the same time, I sent detailed instructions to Marschalk and ordered him to keep me posted every day via the phone.

One day after Kurnatowski and Linder's departure, Marschalk called me and reported that two of the other three thieves who had

---

[31] Imitates speaking Finnish (thirty kopecks) and pronounces Finnish names of two settlements in Russia near St. Petersburg close to the border of Finland

been recognized in hotels of Kharkov were in Moscow and careful surveillance had already been set over them.

So, out of the nine participants, one was in prison in Kharkov, and four, including Kwiatkowski and Goroszek, were permanently watched by Moscow police.

I asked Marschalk to move slowly until I returned, which I thought I would do within the next few days, since I was already feeling better.

Before his departure, I ordered Linder not to stay at the same place Kurnatowski would stay, but instead live in Boyarsky Dvor[32].

This hotel's advantage was that every room had a separate phone in it. My "Hämäläinen" was ordered to live richly, the way a millionaire is supposed to do (which didn't upset him at all), tipping generously, having champagne at lunch, etc.

In about two days, I came to Moscow. It was time to act.

Following my suggestion, Linder lit a pipe and went to Goroszek's lover on Pereyaslavlskaya St., taking with him, of course, the reference letter of the arrested Kharkov official.

For the sake of convenience, in further narration I will call this official Dziewałtowski.

Not only was it forbidden for Linder to see me, but to even come close to Malyi Gnezdnikovsky Lane, i.e., to the police building, where I spent whole days with Marschalk overseeing this case. From our previous experience, we knew how careful and precautious Warsaw thieves were. It was beyond doubt that they would have Hämäläinen shadowed.

So, I looked forward to Linder's phone call regarding his visit to Goroszek's lover. In about three hours, he called and reported:

"I came to the apartment on Pereyaslavlskaya St. and rang the bell; a soubrette opened the door and fixed her eyes on me.

---

[32] Boyarsky Dvor (Russian: Боярский двор, *bo-yar-skiy dvor*), literally meaning 'boyars' yard', is a first-class hotel

"Is Madam home?" I asked her.

"She is, please come in."

I gave her a brand-new business card that read JOHAN CARLOVICH HÄMÄLÄINEN, and under it, in brevier: Helsingfors Exchange Broker.

Shortly, a beautiful young woman came out to the living room to meet me. She raised her eyebrows in surprise and asked:

'Did you wish to see me?'

Distorting my Russian in a Finnish way, I said:

'I was given your address and told that I would find Mr. Kwiatkowski at your place.'

'Kwiatkowski? Who is he?'

'A gentleman, for whom I have a letter from Kharkov, and I would like to see him regarding a very important matter.'

The lady shrugged her shoulders and replied:

'Frankly, I am not sure I can help you. However, I think I heard this name from my brother. Would you please leave your letter here? My brother will come back in two hours or so. Would you be so kind to come back tomorrow at twelve for the response?'

I pretended to hesitate for a little while, but then I gave her Dziewałtowski's letter. While we were talking, the housemaid came into the room to stir the wood in the stove, and I noticed that she was attentively staring at me.

'Hah, there will be some shadowing!' I thought.

Indeed, after I put my coat on, tipped the housemaid a bluey[33], and went outside, I soon noticed a wrapped up silhouette that persistently followed me wherever I went. On my way to the hotel, as a wealthy man, I stopped by a jewelry store, spent about fifte

---

[33] Bills were commonly referred to by their colors. Bluey is the five-ruble bill

minutes there, bought a bulky silver saltshaker with enamel, and went to Boyarsky Dvor with a case in my hands."

"Great, Linder! I am looking forward to your report tomorrow."

On the next day Linder reported:

"I came to the apartment on Pereyaslavlskaya at 12 precisely. This time I was received by two men. They introduced themselves as Kwiatkowski and Goroszek (and they indeed were them) and told me that the madam's brother passed Dziewałtowski's letter to them and provided the apartment to them as a place for negotiations with me.

'When did you come from Helsingfors?' they asked me.

'I came here from Kharkov, where I spent three days,' I replied. 'All this time I spent with Dziewałtowski and his wife. Had dinner at their place three times. Mr. Dziewałtowski asked me to buy interest bearing securities for 2.5 million from you and gave me a letter for you, Mr. Kwiatkowski. By the way, his wife, as she learned that I would meet you, twice asked me insistently to give her sincere and kindest regards to Pan Stanisław.'

After that I looked at Kwiatkowski and gave him a playful smile. He must have been glad about the regards and once and for all gave up his worries about me, identifying me as the 'real' Hämäläinen. After this the conversation turned strictly to business. I said I wanted to see the subject of sale. They said that they didn't have it at the moment and could only show me specimens, about forty thousand's worth. I scrutinized them thoroughly for a long time, gave my approval, and set to haggling. Their first proposal was 2.5 million's worth securities for 2 million cash. I began to protest and assure them that deal would cost me quite a bit. Selling the securities in Russia would be impossible, since they are of course already registered by all the banks and loan institutions as 'illegally acquired'. At the same time, due to the war, Russia was blocked, so delivering them abroad was not an easy thing to do. Finally, we agreed on 1.2 million rubles. After establishing the price, Kwiatkowski and Goroszek said that they would like to be certain and have guarantees of my purchasing power before they bring the subject of sale to Pereyaslavlskaya St. I was about to show them my wallet, tautly stuffed with 'doublets' (packs of pressed newsprint wrapped with five-hundred-ruble bills from both sides), but they only smiled leniently and said:

'This money of course isn't enough!'

'Sure.' I replied. 'But I can't carry 1.2 million rubles around with me, can I?'

'So what do you think to do?' they asked.

I said I would give it some thought and would try to come up with a way to provide them with some kind of guarantee by tomorrow. I also said that unless something delays me I would come to them on the next day, same time."

What was the guarantee that Linder could provide them?

I was searching my mind for quite a while and finally decided to do the following: I went to a post office that was headed by a person I knew, a certain Grigoriev. This post office was situated near Pereyaslavlskaya St.

"I want to ask you for a favor," I said to Grigoriev. "Tomorrow, between noon and 4 p.m., a certain Mr. Hämäläinen will come here, possibly he will not be alone, and he will send a telegram to Helsingfors, to a branch office of Crédit Lyonnais, requesting a transfer of 1.2 million rubles to his current account at the Moscow branch of Volzhsko-Kamsky Bank. Please accept this telegram yourself, but do not send it, of course. Just give it to me later."

Grigoriev promised to carry that out precisely, and I informed Linder of what he was supposed to do next. For things to look more convincing, Linder must have provided in his telegram the address of the place on Pereyaslavlskaya St., where the Helsingfors bank would need to send a notification about the successful transfer.

On the next day, Linder accomplished the plan precisely. He sent a telegram in the presence of Kwiatkowski and asked the latter to immediately notify him on the phone at Boyarsky Dvor once the response from Helsingfors was received.

I went to Grigoriev again, read Linder's telegram that was composed the way I described above, and wrote a response to him right away:

"To Moscow, 14 Pereyaslavlskaya St., Hämäläinen.

Following your request, 1 200 000 (one million two hundred thousand) rubles transferred today to Moscow Volzhsko-Kamsky Bank to your current account No. 13602 (one three six o two)

Crédit Lyonnais Administration."

Grigoriev kindly tapped this text on a paper ribbon, glued it on a telegraph form, left a mark on the side about the sender's location (Helsingfors) and date and hour of sending, sealed the telegram, and gave it to me. The next morning agent Patapkin, disguised as a mailman, went to Pereyaslavlskaya St., passed the telegram, and even got a three rubles tip.

Linder waited for the notification on the phone.

However, the day ended, and no-one called him. I was worried already and didn't sleep well that night, but in the morning Linder called me:

"Sir, I was notified about the telegram, it was forwarded, and they told me to come to Pereyaslavlskaya by two o'clock for the completion of the deal."

Linder's voice was somewhat cheerless.

"What's with you, Linder? Are you afraid?"

"I can't hide it. It's kinda scary! Think about it, sir. They think I will arrive with 1.2 million rubles, so what if it occurs to the swindlers to kill me and rob me?"

"Nonsense. Like you don't know that professional thieves of their caliber are not icemen (killers). Unless it's self-defense."

"That's true, but I still feel a bit frightened! Who knows?"

"Keep your chin up, Linder, and remember that one doesn't get promoted without trying hard. Here's what I want to know: Is the hall of the apartment on Pereyaslavlskaya close to the living room where you're usually received?"

"Quite close. They're next to each other."

"Can you see the street and the driveway through the living room's windows?"

"Yes, the last window looks out on the driveway."

"Great! In an hour, an agent will come to you, disguised as a salesman of the jewelry store where you bought the saltshaker the other day.

He will bring you a case with a thing that you allegedly ordered and will ask to see you personally. Memorize his appearance.

Tomorrow this agent will be standing to the right of the entrance of your hotel at 11:30 a.m., disguised as a cabman. You will take his cab to go to the bank and to Pereyaslavlskaya. I will send you the instructions for tomorrow with this salesman. Discussing it on the phone would take a lot of time and wouldn't be safe. Besides, this way rules out the possibility of a mistake. You will have enough time to acquaint yourself with the plan. Well, goodbye, Linder. I wish you full success, and do not forget about your upcoming reward."

I hung up and set to writing.

"At twelve o'clock sharp, leave your hotel and take the cab that will be waiting for you to the right of the entrance. Go to Volzhsko-Kamsky bank and come up to its entrance with an empty briefcase under your arm. At the bank, you will be received by an agent who will come to you today at eight in the evening as your acquaintance (memorize his face well). Somewhere in a bathroom of the bank he will stuff your briefcase with twelve five-hundred-ruble-bill 'doublets,' each of them looking like a pack of 100 thousand rubles. After spending an hour at least at the bank, come out of it, looking around worriedly and carrying the full briefcase under your arm. The cabman will take you to Pereyaslavlskaya and will stay there, waiting for you on the driveway. In case they do not have the 'subject of sale' with them, contrary to our expectation, curse a little bit or behave according to the situation, but do not raise an alarm, and just go home looking upset. If they say they do have the subject of sale, make sure they do, and set to examination. Inspecting securities and tickets will probably take you about two hours. During the examination, pretend to be worried that the cabman may leave, so come up to the window, knock on the glass loudly, and shake your finger at the cabman when he looks at you; try to show him with your actions that he must wait for you even if you're delayed till evening. The cabman will show you that he is cold and will hit his hands against each other and tap himself on the shoulders, which will be the signal for Kurnatowski, who will be on duty across the street. Exactly thirty minutes after this signal, Kurnatowski with a dozen of agents will break into the apartment and arrest everyone there. It would be preferable, but not necessary, for you to go to the hall under some pretense and secretly unlock the door that opens to the staircase. That would make it easier for Kurnatowski and his people to get into the living room as quickly as possible.

However, in case you can't do it, the door will be broken open in no time.

I order you to stick to this plan most strictly. Only insignificant details of your behavior may be altered according to your discretion, but generally they must comply with the foregoing."

I gave this set of instructions to an agent and sent him to Linder, to Boyarsky Dvor.

By two o'clock of the next day, Pereyaslavlskaya St. was teeming with agents. Four yard keepers with brooms and crowbars were breaking ice and clearing it away, three cabmen were bustling around, a newsboy on the corner was crying out the newspaper's titles, on the other corner a pauper was begging, a Tatar man with a bundle behind his back was slowly walking around the yards, shouting plaintively, "A robe, a robe for sale!" and L. A. Kurnatowski was sitting in a beerhouse opposite to the building that was under surveillance, melancholically sipping his beer from a mug. All those people, of course, were armed with Brownings.

At two o'clock precisely, the cabman flew up to the driveway. He hardly managed to rein the trotter in.

Linder came out of the sledge with the briefcase in his hands, worriedly looked around, and finally entered the building. "It had been about an hour, I guess," Kurnatowski told me afterwards. "I kept looking at the cabman. Finally I saw this coachman clap his mittens and then tap his shoulders crosswise, swaying back and forth in a measured manner. I looked at my clock: It was five minutes to three. At twenty-five past three exactly I left the beerhouse, gave a signal to my people and quickly broke into the building with about ten agents who had run up to me.

The apartment's door was unlocked, so we ran through the hall and stormed into the living room. Before Linder had time to exclaim with fake amazement something like 'ter-r-rijoki![34]', the tables were overturned, papers were scattered, and Kwiatkowski and Goroszek were put down on the floor, disarmed, and handcuffed. In this mess, Linder had a hard time, too, since he kept crying out Finnish swearwords.

There was no need for a search. All of the stolen interest-bearing securities were right there."

I had been very worried, sitting in the police station, waiting for the end of Linder's purchase. The time went by so slowly. I was trying to picture what was going on there. It's two o'clock, Linder hasn't called, so the "subject of sale," I should think, was there. It's four o'clock, so probably the cabman has already given the signal, so Kurnatowski is getting ready to break in.

Maybe he already has?

Around five, I heard a noise and the stomping of many feet. Entering my office were Kurnatowski with agents and Kwiatkowski, Goroszek and Linder under arrest. Kurnatowski had a briefcase in his hands.

"So, Lyudovik Antonovich, is all the money there?"

"Yes, Arkady Frantsevich, all of it."

"Well, thank God!"

Goroszek and Kwiatkowski were looking at Linder with embarrassment the entire time, like they were apologizing for getting him into trouble unintentionally. However, it wasn't for long, because Linder turned to me and said:

"Sir, please give the command to take these damn handcuffs off! My hands are numb already."

---

[34] Finnish name of another settlement near St. Petersburg

I smiled, ordered that Linder be freed and offered him a seat. When they saw this and heard his flawless Russian pronunciation, the Poles looked extremely confused, gaped at him and goggled their eyes.

After listening to Kurnatowski's brief report, I asked Linder to tell us about his last visit.

"Well, sir, I came to Pereyaslavlskaya at two o'clock sharp, took off my coat, but entered the living room with this white and green knitted scarf wrapped around my neck. I apologized for it and said, 'Oh, this Moscow of yours! I just arrived and already caught a cold, and a cough, and a runny nose!—Moscow isn't Warsaw, and the climate here isn't ours!'

After that Goroszek and Kwiatkowski persistently offered me a glass of wine to the upcoming deal. They pulled me toward a little table with several brands of champagne on it, expensive fruit and candies. I resolutely refused and said that business came first and drinks were to come after.

They didn't insist too much, and soon we took our seats. I was on the one side of two open card tables moved together, and Kwiatkowski and Goroszek were on the other side.

'Before we start with the examination, I would like to see the subject of sale in full, and I believe you would like to see the money. That's why I'm asking you to lay all the securities out on the table, and concerning the money, here it is,' I opened my briefcase, quickly poured its content on the table, and then put the packs back. Kwiatkowski went to another room, brought another briefcase, then took packs of securities out of it, and put them on the table. We took pencils and sheets of paper, and the examination started. I was trying to make it as slow as I could: I scrutinized every paper, wrote down its number, checked tickets, etc. Fortunately, the securities were of rather little value, most of them for 5 and 10 thousand, so there really were many of them. After examining about 500 thousand's worth of them, I settled back in the armchair, coughed, looked at my watch, and pretended to be horrified. 'Oh my God! It's three o'clock already, and only less than a quarter has been examined!' Then I tried to look worried, saying, 'I hope my fool out there won't leave!' I got up, hurriedly came up to the window, knocked on the glass loudly, and expressively shook my finger at the cabman. Then I took my seat again and continued examination, coughing every once in a while. In about twenty minutes, I faked a new, acute attack of coughing, so strong it even made my eyes water, and dipped my fingers in my pocket to get the handkerchief.

It wasn't there. 'I guess it's in my coat,' I said, quickly got up before my sellers knew it, and went out to the hall, my briefcase with me all the time. I looked back: No-one followed me. So I unsnapped the French lock on the door, took the handkerchief and came back to the living room, having it pressed to my lips. We continued, but in less than ten minutes, our people suddenly broke in from the hall, so we were knocked down, disarmed and pinioned. By the way, sir, could you give a command to give my Browning back to me?"

The Poles listened to Linder's story without tearing their eyes away from him, and in the end of it Kwiatkowski exclaimed:

"Jak Boga kocham[35], good job! What can I say? I could bet he wasn't Russian, but a Finn! And then again, with regards from Pani Dziewałtowska, and the telegram, and the money, and we followed him when he went to the bank today.... But you didn't know we were watching you, did you?"

"I did! I knew it, Pan Kwiatkowski." Linder replied. "That's what makes us experienced detectives. We know everything! You, guest performers from Warsaw, do a very fine job, but the way we catch you is even finer."

Kwiatkowski clicked his tongue and shook his head in perplexity.

"Don't be angry with us, gentlemen, in case my people gave you a hard time during the arrest," I said. "But you must understand that under these circumstances it's inevitable."

"Please, sir, we have no complaints. How can it be otherwise? We snatch, you catch; every man does his business. It's a pity though that everything failed so suddenly. But we'll make up for it, let us assure you!"

---

[35] I swear to God (Polish)

"Tell me please, would you give me the addresses of the seven other participants of the affair?"

"No, sir, we won't. We're caught, and the money is found, so let it be. But we're not giving up anyone."

"That's certainly up to you. But I hope we'll find them without your assistance."

I ordered the immediate arrest of the two thieves that Marschalk told me about on the phone when I was in Petrograd. They had been watched by the police the whole time. By the end of the day, three more participants were arrested. They ran into an ambush that had been laid in the apartment on Pereyaslavlskaya. Therefore, including Dziewałtowski, we arrested eight people out of nine. The ninth one disappeared without a trace and wasn't found before the February Revolution.

Upon completion of this much-discussed investigation, the participants of it were showered with rewards. Lapsin, the assistant to the chief of the Kharkov police, was granted a monetary reward, Linder was promoted, and Kurnatowski received the fourth class Order of Saint Vladimir.

This is how our merits were awarded by the Imperial Government. The Provisional Government awarded us in a different fashion. During its time, the prison doors opened wide to let out all kinds of rogues and to place the likes of us in them. Poor Kurnatowski, who faced the Revolution in the position of the chief of the Kharkov police, to which he was promoted two weeks after this theft was solved, was put into that same Kharkov prison, where he met Goroszek, Kwiatkowski and the other participants of the bank theft. For the sake of justice, I must say that they showed no schadenfreude, nor did they take vengeance on Kurnatowski; generally, their behavior was dramatically different from that of our Russian thieves. I interceded with Prince G. E. Lvov[36], and as a result Kurnatowski was freed. After spending about a year more in Russia, he finally immigrated to Poland, where until this day he works as either the chief or the assistant chief of the Warsaw Criminal Investigation

---

[36] Georgy Lvov was the prime minister of Russia in March—July 1917

Department. Marschalk and Linder also languished in Sovdepia[37] for a certain amount of time, but then moved to Warsaw, and now, as far I know, they have their own businesses.

Concerning your most humble servant, he made his way in autumn of 1918 to the hetman[38] in Kiev. When Skoropadskyi fell and Petliura[39] came, I attempted to leave Kiev twice, but both times I was pulled off the train by Petliura's troops. I was stuck in Kiev, and that is where I was during the Bolshevik invasion.

Once during those gloomy days, I was wandering along Khreshchatyk[40]. Suddenly I heard a voice:

"Pan Koshko, is that really you?"

I raised my head and saw Kwiatkowski and Goroszek before me.

I was stupefied. I thought my story was over. They would definitely give me up to the Bolsheviks!

But Kwiatkowski, as he saw my confusion, said:

"Calm down, Pan Koshko. We bear no grudge against you, and we hate Bolsheviks just as much as you do."

Then they looked at my threadbare clothes and considerately offered:

"Do you maybe need some money? I will loan you some with no problems."

I said no. He smiled and said,

---

[37] A disparaging term for Soviet Russia

[38] Pavlo Skoropadskyi, Hetman of Ukraine, was the state leader of Ukraine in April—December 1918 and bore the title

[39] Symon Petliura was the chairman of the Directorate of the Ukrainian People's Republic in 1919-1926

[40] Khreshchatyk is the main central street of Kiev

"Possibly you think that the money is stolen? No, we quit. Now we're into fair business."

Of course, I refused their "fair" money, but I must say that I was profoundly moved by these people, which I openly told them.

From Kiev, I moved to Odessa, then to Crimea, then to Constantinople, and, finally, to Paris. But the time of my work as the head of criminal police in Crimea as well as my private agency of criminal investigation in Constantinople possibly will be the subject of the second volume of my memoirs.

Copyright © 2015 New York Concept

All rights reserved. No part of this book may be used or reproduced in any manner whatsoever without a written permission. For information regarding permission, please, contact at books@nyc-books.com.

Written by **A. F. Koshko**

Translated by **S. Viatchanin**

Edited by **Merrell Knighten**, **Joanna Rempel Knighten**

Cover Picture - **LehaKok**

Cover Design – **Lauria**

Thank you for purchasing this New York Concept Book!

Sign up for our newsletter and receive new releases for **Free** at **www.nyc-books.com**

Contact us for any inquiries at **books@nyc-books.com** or **https://twitter.com/nyc_publisher**

*****

Finally, before you go, we'd like to say thank you for purchasing this book. If you find it entertaining and useful, could you, please, take a minute and *leave a review* and share your thoughts on social media?

Your feedback will help us continue to publish books for children, young adults and parents.

Turn the page for a preview of immortal classic dystopian novel

WE

Yevgeny Zamyatin
Introduction by George Orwell
Translation, Summary and Analysis
by S. Viatchanin

Entry 1

Abstract: Announcement. The Wisest of Lines. A Poem

I am simply copying, verbatim, what was published in the State Newspaper today:

"THE *INTEGRAL* construction is to be complete in 120 days. The great historic hour is coming when the first *INTEGRAL* will soar into outer space. A thousand years ago, our heroic ancestors brought the entire world under control of the One State. You are about to accomplish an even more glorious feat: integrating the Universe's infinite equation with the glass, electric, fire-breathing *INTEGRAL*. You are about to proceed with bending the unknown creatures inhabiting other planets, possibly still in the savage state of freedom, to the beneficent yoke of reason. In case they do not understand we are bringing them mathematically faultless happiness, our duty is to make them be happy. Before we take arms, though, we shall try words.

On the behalf of the Benefactor, it is announced to all the numbers of the One State:

Anyone who feels capable of composing treatises, poems, manifestos, odes and other works praising the beauty and greatness of the One State must do so.

These works will be the first cargo the *INTEGRAL* will carry.

Long live the One State, long live numbers, long live the Benefactor!"

As I write this, I feel my cheeks burning. Yes: Integrate the grand universal equation. Yes: Unbend the savage curve, straighten it tangentially, asymptotically, correctly, for the line of the One State is a straight line. A great, divine, accurate, and wise straight line—the wisest of lines...

I am D-503, a constructor of the *Integral*, merely one of the mathematicians of the One State. Accustomed to digits, my pen is unable to create the music of assonances and rhymes. I attempt only to record what I see and think—or rather what *we* think (it is indeed "we," and may *WE* be the title of my records). But this writing will be a derivative of our life, of the One State's mathematically perfect life, so will it not turn out a poem in its nature beyond my control? It will—I believe and I know.

As I write this, I feel my cheeks burning. It must feel like what a woman experiences when she hears the pulse of a new, yet tiny, blind little person within herself for the first time. This is me and yet not myself at the same time. For months I will have to nourish it with my sap, my blood, and then painfully tear it off myself and lay it at the One State's feet.

But I am ready, just like every, or almost every, one of us. I am ready.

Entry 2

Abstract: Ballet, Square Harmony. X

Springtime. From beyond the Green Wall, from invisible wildernesses, the wind carries the yellow honey powder of flowers of various kinds. This sweet powder makes the lips parched, so you have to wipe them with your tongue every minute. Every woman you meet must have sweet lips (and surely every man as well). It somehow hinders logical thinking.

But the sky! Blue and unspoiled with a single cloud (how savage was the taste of ancient people, if their poets could find inspiration in awkward, untidy, and inanely jostling piles of vapor). I like—I am sure I will not make a mistake saying—*we* like the sky only like this, sterile and flawless. On days like this, the whole world is cast in the same inviolable and eternal glass as the Green Wall, as all of our buildings are cast in. On days like this, one can see the very depth of things, their amazing equations that had thitherto been unknown—one can see them in something that is so habitual and every day.

Take this as an example: This morning I was in the hangar where the *Integral* is being constructed, and I suddenly saw the machinery—eyes closed, self-forgetfully, the regulators' spheres were spinning; glittering cranks were bending left and right; the balance beam was proudly swaying its shoulders; the slotter's bit was dropping, following an unheard music's rhythm. I suddenly saw the entire beauty of this grand machine's ballet flooded with the light-blue sky.

I then asked myself: Why is that so beautiful? Why is the dance beautiful? The answer was: Because the motion is unfree, because the whole deep meaning of the dance is about absolute and esthetical dependence, about perfect unfreedom. If it is true that our ancestors would give themselves up to dancing in the most inspired moments of their lives (religious mysteries, military parades), it means precisely that the instinct of unfreedom is organically inherent in human beings from the earliest times, so in our present life we consciously—

I will have to finish later: My numerator just clicked. I am looking up: It is O-90, of course. In thirty seconds she will be here to take me out for a walk.

Sweet O! I always thought she resembled her name: about ten centimeters shorter than the Mother Norm, rounded off, with her pink O-like mouth open to every word I say. And more: a round plump little fold on her wrist, just like that of a child.

When she entered, the logic flywheel was still dinning in me at its top speed, so I automatically started talking about the formula I had just figured out that included all of us, and the machines, and dancing.

"Marvelous, isn't it?" I asked.

"It is. It's spring," O-90 smiled to me pinkly.

Well, how about that: It's spring ... She is talking about the spring. Women ... I fell silent.

Downstairs. The avenue is full: In such weather, we usually spend the personal hour after lunch in an extra walk. As always, the Musical Factory was singing the One State March with all its pipes, and in measured rows, four in each, enthusiastically beating time, the numbers were marching. Hundreds, thousands of numbers wearing light-bluish unifs[41] with golden nameplates on their chests—state numbers of every one.

And I—the four of us—constitute one of the countless waves in this mighty stream. To my left is O-90 (if this had been written by one of my hairy ancestors about a thousand years ago, he would have probably called her the funny word *my*); to my right are two numbers I do not know, a female one and a male one.

Blissfully blue sky, tiny baby suns in each of the nameplates, and faces unshadowed by the madness of thoughts .... Rays—you see, everything is made of the same radiant and smiling matter. And the brass time, "Ra-tah-tah-tam. Ra-tah-tah-tam," and the copper steps shining under the sun, and getting higher and higher with every step, into the breathtaking blue ....

And just the way it was this morning in the hangar I saw again, as if for the first time in my life, I saw everything: unalterable straight streets, the glass pavement splashing rays of light, divine parallelepipeds of transparent dwellings, the square harmony of grey-blue ranks. And it feels as though it was not generations, but it was me, just me, who defeated the old God and old life, me who created all this, and I feel like a tower; I am afraid of moving my elbows so that walls, domes and machines do not shatter ....

In the next moment I jump through centuries, from '+' to '−'. I remembered—it must be association by contrast—I suddenly remembered a picture in a museum. Their avenue of the old days, back in the 20th century, with deafeningly motley and tangled crowds of people, wheels, animals, posters, trees, colors, and birds .... And it is believed that such things actually existed—could exist. I found it so implausible and ridiculous I could not help bursting into sudden laughter.

I immediately heard an echoing laughter to the right. I turned my head: Before my eyes were white, unbelievably white and sharp teeth and an unknown female face.

---

[41] Most likely comes from ancient word 'uniforme'

"Excuse me," she said. "It is just you have been viewing everything around in such an inspired manner like some kind of a mythical god on the seventh day of creation. It seems to me you are sure that I too was created by you and not anyone else. It is very flattering."

None of this was said with a smile, but rather with a sort of respectfulness (she might know that I was a constructor for the *Integral*). But there was—I am not sure if in the eyes or in the eyebrows some strange, annoying X that I could not capture or give a mathematical expression.

For some reason I felt embarrassed and started (not too smoothly) trying to justify my laughter logically. It is absolutely clear that this contrast, the impassable abyss between today and back then—

"Why is that impassible?" (Such white teeth!) "A bridge can be thrown across an abyss. Imagine: drums, battalions, ranks—all these actually took place, therefore ...."

"Well yes, it's obvious!" I cried (that was an astonishing coincidence of thoughts. She expressed, with almost exact same word, what I had been writing down before the walk). "You see: even the thoughts. That is because it is not 'one,' but 'one of.' We are so alike—"

She: "Are you sure?"

I saw eye-brows lifted at an acute angle to temples, like little horns of an X, and I lost my train of thought again for some reason. I looked right, looked left, and ....

To my right—she, slim, sharp, stubbornly lithe like a whip, I-330 (I can see her number now); and to my left—O, completely different, all made of curves, with the childish little fold on her wrist, and in the end of our four, a male number I didn't know, some double-bent one looking like an S. We were all different.

The one to the right, I-330, must have caught my confused glance, and she sighed.

"Well ... alas!"

As a matter of fact, this "alas" was absolutely appropriate. But there was something again in her face or her voice ....

I was unusually harsh when I said:

"No reason for 'alas.' The science grows and it is obvious that if not now, then in fifty or a hundred years—"

"Even everybody's noses are—"

"Yes, noses," I was almost shouting. "If any, there is no difference what the ground for envy is .... If mine is button-shaped, and someone else's—"

"Well, your nose, I could even say, is a 'classic' one, as they used to say in the times of old. But the hands .... No, show me, show me your hands!"

I hate it when somebody looks at my hands: all hairy and shaggy. A ridiculous atavism.

I put my hand out and said as indifferently as I could:

"Like ape's."

She looked at my hands, then in my face.

"This is a very curious chord." She was estimating me, like weighing me on a scale, and the little horns in the corners of her eyebrows showed again.

"He is registered with me," O-90 opened her mouth joyfully and pinkly.

I wish she had kept silence—what she said was a very improper thing to say. Generally sweet O ... how do I say this ... the speed of her tongue is not correctly adjusted. The speed of tongue should always be a bit lower than the speed of thinking, not the other way around.

In the end of the avenue, on the Accumulator Tower, the bell was boomingly ringing 17. The personal hour was over. I-330 was leaving with the S-like male number. His face commands respect, and, as I see now, looks familiar. I had met him somewhere before—I cannot remember now.

Before we parted, I smiled at me crookedly in the same X manner.

"Stop by auditorium one-twelve the day after tomorrow."

I shrugged my shoulders.

"If I am assigned to the auditorium you are referring to—"

With some mysterious certainty, she said: "You will be."

This woman was affecting me the unpleasant way that an indecomposable irrational term affects an equation it accidentally smuggled into, so I was glad to be with sweet O for at least a bit of time.

Arm in arm, we passed four lines of avenues together. On the corner she was to turn right, and I was to turn left.

"I would like so much to come over to your place today, draw the curtains. Today, just now ...." O looked up at me with her rounded blue-crystal eyes.

Funny her. What could I say? She had stayed at my place the day before and she knew for sure that our next sexual day would be the day after tomorrow. It was the same "ahead of thinking" thing of hers, like the (sometimes harmful) phenomenon of premature generation of a spark in an engine.

Two ... no, I should be precise: Three times I kissed her marvelous blue unspoiled by even a single little cloud eyes goodbye.

Entry 3

Abstract: A jacket. The Wall. The Tablet

I scanned what had been written yesterday, and I see that I did not write clearly enough. I mean all of this is perfectly clear to any one of us. But who knows: Maybe you, the unfamiliar ones the *Integral* will bring my records to, have read the book of civilization only till the page where our ancestors stopped 900 or so years ago. Maybe you do not even know the basics like The Time Tablet, Personal Hours, the Mother Norm, the Green Wall, the Benefactor. It is ridiculous and very hard for me at the same time to explain it. It is the same difficulty that a writer from, say, the 20th century would have in explaining in his novel what "a jacket" is, or "a flat," or "a wife." If his novel is to be translated for barbarians, can it possibly get along without a comment on "jacket"?

I am sure that a barbarian would take a look at the "jacket" and think, "What's that for anyway? Nothing but a burden." It seems to me that you will take an exactly same look at me when I tell you that none of us has gone beyond the Green Wall since the Two Hundred Years' War.

But dear, you should give it some thought—it is really helpful. It is clear that the entire history of mankind, as far as we are aware of it, is the history of transition from nomadic forms to more and more settled ones. Does this not mean, therefore, that the most settled way of life (ours) is as well the perfect one (ours). If people ever rushed around the earth back and forth, it happened back in pre-historic times, when there were nations, wars, commerce, and the discovery of Americas of all sorts. Who might need it now and what for?

I concede: The habit of such a settled lifestyle was not formed easily or straight away. When all the roads were destroyed and became overgrown with grass during the Two Hundred Years' War, it must have seemed quite inconvenient to live in cities cut off from each other with green thickets. Well, what of it? After the first humans' tails fell off, it must have taken them a while to learn how to keep flies off without the tail. No doubt, they missed the tail at first, but now, can you imagine having a tail? Or, say, can you imagine being outdoors naked, without your "jacket" on (in case you happen to still sport "jackets")? This is exactly the case: I cannot imagine a city not wearing its Green Wall. I cannot imagine life that wouldn't be clothed in the digital vestment of The Tablet.

The Tablet .... In this same moment its purple digits against the gold background are looking into my eyes sternly and tenderly from the wall in my room. I cannot help thinking about the thing that the ancients called "icon," and it makes me want to make verses and prayers (which are essentially the same). Ah, why am I not a poet who would deserve to sing your praises, o Tablet, o heart and pulse of the One State?

As kids back in school, all of us (and, possibly, you as well) read the greatest surviving work of ancient literature: the Train Schedule. But even that, put next to The Tablet, would be graphite next to a diamond. They both contain the same, C, carbon, but how eternal, how limpid the diamond is, how brightly it shines. Whose breath would not be taken by rushing and crashing through the Schedule's pages? But The Tablet in reality turns each of us into a great epic poem's six-wheeled hero made of steel. Every morning, six-wheeled-precise, at the same hour and the same minute, we, millions of us, get up as one. At the same time we start working, millions as one, and we finish, again millions as one. Having merged into a single million-handed body at the same second scheduled by The Tablet, we raise our spoons to our mouths, and it is the same second we go for a walk, and go to the auditorium, and to the Taylor exercise hall, and go to bed ....

I should be as frank as possible: Even we do not yet have the absolutely accurate solution for this problem of happiness. Twice a day, 16 to 17 and 21 to 22, the one mighty organism breaks down into separate cells; those are Personal Hours scheduled by The Tablet. During these hours you will see that some have their curtains virtuously drawn; others measuredly walk down the avenue on the copper steps of the March; others, like me at the moment, are at their desks. But I strongly believe, though I may be called an idealist and a dreamer, that sooner or later, some day we will find the place for these hours in the general formula. Some day all 86,400 seconds of the day will make it to The Time Tablet.

I happened to read and hear a lot of unbelievable things about the times when people lived in a free, i.e. unorganized, savage state. But this very thing always seemed the most unbelievable to me: How could the state power then, as rudimentary as it was, permit people to live without anything like our Tablet, without compulsory walks, without precise regulation of food timing, to get up and go to bed whenever they wanted. Some historians even say that back then lights would be on in the streets all night long, and all night people would walk and drive around the streets.

I still cannot comprehend it. No matter how limited their reasoning was, they must have understood that leading lives like this was murder—just a slow one, day by day. The state (humanity) would prohibit killing one person, but did not prohibit killing millions of people by halves? Killing a person, i.e. reducing the total of human lives by 50 years, is a crime, while reducing the total of human lives by 50 millions of years is not a crime? How ridiculous is that? Here this mathematically moral problem can be solved in 30 seconds by any 10-year-old; there nobody could solve it, not even all their Kants combined (because none of Kants was smart enough to create a system of scientific ethics, i.e., one based on subtraction, addition, division, and multiplication).

Is it not absurd that a state (how dared it call itself a state!) could leave sexual life completely uncontrolled? Whoever, whenever, as much as they wanted ... absolutely unscientific, just like animals. And just like animals, blindly, they would have children. Is it not ridiculous: to be familiar with gardening, poultry-breeding, fish-breeding (we possess definite data confirming they were familiar with these) and fail to make it to the last step of this logical ladder: child-breeding, and not to be smart enough to invent the Mother Norm and the Father Norm we have.

It is so ridiculous and so implausible that now that I have written this, I am afraid that you, unfamiliar readers, could think me to be a mean joker. What if you think that I simply want to make fun of you and tell you complete nonsense while pretending to be serious?

But, first, I am not capable of joking, for in every joke, a lie enters like an implicit function. And second, the One State Science affirms that the life of the ancient people was exactly like this, and the One State Science cannot be wrong. Anyway, how could state logic possibly come about in that time when people lived in the state of freedom, that is of animals, of apes, of a herd? What can we demand of them, if even now sometimes, from somewhere below, from the shaggy depths, a wild, apelike echo is heard.

Fortunately, it is seldom. Fortunately, those are only minor accidents with small parts: They are easily repaired without having to stop the eternal and great work of the entire Machine. For throwing a bent bolt away, we have the clever and firm hand of the Benefactor, and we have experienced eyes of the Guards.

And before I forget: the double-bent S-like man I met yesterday—I think I saw him coming out of the Bureau of Guards one day. I now understand how I got that instinctive feeling of respect toward him and some awkwardness, when I-330 was around him. I must confess: this I-330 ....

It's ringing to go to sleep: it is 22.30. Till tomorrow.

BUY AT http://amzn.to/1hq8kG3

Printed in Great Britain
by Amazon

21528799R00129